Big, Bold, Brave will help you align your dreams, goals, and habits. You will find your breakthrough within these hands-on experiences. Written from the heart, the life lessons in this book contain the power to change the course of your life!
Hans Gijsbertsen, Founder and CEO at Bonjoy

I'm convinced that nothing impacts the heart and brings greater transformation than a story. No fact or statistic is more convincing than a story. And the greatest stories seem to have had the greatest cost. Clint gives you a powerful story, his family's story, that came at the greatest cost. He has mined deep into the cave of his pain to bring forth gold for all of us. After reading his book, I discovered how fear was affecting my own life in parenting—consciously and subconsciously limiting my own adult kids. Not anymore. Clint's book and response to pain has transformed that part of me to keep inspiring those I love to live *Big, Bold and Brave*.
Me Ra Koh, Co-Founder of FIORIA

Big, Bold, and Brave is a compelling call for us to step up and out - to follow the call God has for each of us, and to pursue it with urgency. Clint reminds us that tomorrow is not promised, so live on purpose today. I appreciate Clint's vulnerability, emotion, honesty, and courage. Clint will challenge you to reflect, assess, and commit to becoming your best version of yourself day to day. I was moved by Clint's story, words, and courage, and know others will be as well.
David Hollie, District Manager, Starbucks

Clint's ability to communicate the heartbreaking, life changing emotions of having a great loss in life is very touching. *Big, Bold and Brave* is inspirational and should help the reader live a more positive, productive life, with less fear. The book is captivating, easy to read and understand. The book makes me feel better equipped to help my patients through traumatic events that have occurred in their lives.
J. M. Stanton, DO, FAOCA
Chief of Staff,
Baylor, Scott and White Medical Center-
Trophy Club

Clint is a top-shelf communicator with an uncanny ability to articulate some of life's most complex issues. He has a unique way of leading his readers to incredible ah-ha moments. *Big, Bold, and Brave* gives language and Solomon-like wisdom to one of the deepest mysteries of our human experience—personal tragedy. I was taken on a journey through raw emotions and disappointment into a land full of hope and a future. Quite frankly, my belief system will never be the same. Thank you, Clint, for making the veil between heaven and earth much thinner.
Ray Goolsby, BETHEL LEADERS NETWORK *BLN Coach*

There are some educational courses that we would never sign up for by choice. The assignment that was given to this family is one of those. The trial of losing a child, an outstanding, gifted, and high achieving child, is one of the most difficult journeys we can walk through. I have watched this family walk through this journey with the pain and process that would be expected. The difference is that many do not survive. Clint Hatton came through this challenge and wrote a book about it. A book that allows all of us a look inside the painful process and teach us the way to come out boldly and walking in victory. In *Big, Bold and Brave*, Clint offers us a gift. You can read the book and learn the lesson of it to better prepare you for a life that can come at us hard. I believe we will all be better after joining the Hattons on this journey.
Mike Hayes, Founder
Churches in Covenant International

Life is short. If you've ever lost a loved one you know exactly how precious and short life really is. Yet, most of us go through life playing it safe, letting our fears get the best of us, and allowing them to prevent us from living a life of peace, purpose, and love. Author, Clint Hatton, knows all too well the pain of loss after losing his teenage son in 2019, yet despite the tragedy, he decided to confront the fear and live a courageous life. He shares powerful lessons and heartfelt stories of his journey along the way, and how he *chose* to give his pain a purpose by *choosing* to live *Big Bold Brave*. If he can do it, you can too!"
Michelle Prince, CEO
Performance Publishing Group
PerformancePublishingGroup.com

It's a book everyone who doubts if God is real needs to read. It's a journey in experiencing God's hand on a family during their great trials as He brings them through it. The outcome is a life of love, understanding, and peace. A great read.
Ola B. Madsen, Founder and President
Adventures in Total Development, LLC
OlaMadsen.me

Clint takes the reader on an incredibly powerful journey through his own family's trials to show us all that *Big, Bold, Brave* is the only choice to make in dealing with life's trials and tribulations! It was just what I needed - a must read!!
John Albers, President/CEO, Albers Aerospace

FOREWORD BY
HOWARD BEHAR
Retired President, *Starbucks* International

BIG
BOLD
BRAVE

How to Live Courageously in a Risky World

CLINT HATTON

Copyright © 2022
Clint Hatton

Performance Publishing Group
McKinney, TX

All Worldwide Rights Reserved.
All rights reserved. No part of this publication may be reproduced, stored in a retrieval system or transmitted, in any form or by any means, electronic, mechanical, recorded, photocopied, or otherwise, without the prior written permission of the copyright owner, except by a reviewer who may quote brief passages in a review.

ISBN:
Softcover: 978-1-956914-93-1
Hardcover: 978-1-956914-78-8
eBook: 978-1-956914-73-3

Contents

Acknowledgements ix
Foreword xi
Introduction xv

Chapter 1: Our Worst Nightmare 1
Chapter 2: Life or Death 13
Chapter 3: Perfectly Imperfect 31
Chapter 4: Your Life Message 41
Chapter 5: The FedEx Guy 55
Chapter 6: Peace: A Guide Through the Chaos 67
Chapter 7: A Lesson in Collaboration 79
Chapter 8: Fear, Less! 93
Chapter 9: Courageous Decisions 111
Chapter 10: Giving Pain a Purpose 119
Chapter 11: What Do You Really Want? 137
Chapter 12: Parasites and Boundaries 155

My Why 163

Dedication

To my son, Gabriel. This book exists because of the way you *lived*. Simple words fail to adequately express how much we miss your presence. You are in our hearts and thoughts daily. The legacy you left in your wake will change countless lives. For me, mom, Joel, and Liam, you will always be the symbol of what it means to live Big, Bold, and Brave. Love, Dad.

Gabriel's Senior Photo Shoot 2018
Photo Credit: FIORIA by Me Ra Koh

Acknowledgements

To my gorgeous bride, Amárillys. I am eternally grateful to be on this journey with you. This book would have never made it to print without your love, grace, input, editing prowess, encouragement, and willingness to take risks.

To my sons, Joel, and Liam. I am so proud of how courageously you have lived these last few years. You are both warriors. Mom and I are blessed to call you sons. We are inspired every day by the way *you* attack life. There are no limits to what either of you will accomplish.

To Blake Steinecke, Robert Kasozi, Daryl Davis, and Colby and Caroline Harries. Thank you for allowing me to share your stories. I believe each of you have and will change millions of lives! I am honored to collaborate with you.

To Howard Behar. Though many others have provoked me to write this project, your insistence that it was the right time to do so was the final catalyst in my putting pen to paper. I am thankful for your continued support and the foreword to this book!

Lastly, I would like to thank my publisher, Michelle Prince, and her team at Performance Publishing Group for making it easy to think I could write this book! It was a labor of love.

Foreword

FOR OVER FIFTY years I have been a devoted student and teacher of the Servant Leadership Model and a passionate advocate for leading with purpose. Part of that model—and of my life philosophy—is that each of us should only wear *one hat* in life. I propose that when you try to wear multiple hats (i.e., you function differently depending on the role), the result is a dilution of your true self. You may function in many roles, but you are a whole human being. Our personal hat is a metaphor for being consistent with oneself. One-hat leadership is synonymous with honesty, clarity, passion, and a sense of being truly engaged and alive.

I have been fortunate to have the opportunity to influence others by wearing my one hat in all my roles as a husband, father, grandfather, business executive, speaker, advisor, mentor, and bestselling author. For 21 years I had the privilege of leading Starbucks' domestic business as their President of North American operations. I eventually became the founding President of Starbucks International, opening the very first store outside of North America in Japan.

With the Servant Leadership Model as my catalyst, I participated in the growth of the company from only 28 stores to over 15,000 across five continents. I continued to serve on the Starbucks Board of Directors for twelve years before retiring. I do my best to live by this model today. Since the successful publication of my first book, *It's Not About the*

FOREWORD

Coffee: Lessons on Leadership from a Life at Starbucks (Portfolio, 2008), I have enjoyed traveling the world and speaking to and connecting with leaders, organizations, and students who are uniquely positioned to carry the message of servant leadership forward.

I first connected with Clint Hatton after I had been a guest on *The Ed Mylett Show*. Clint reached out through email, expressing gratitude for the content of the podcast and relaying his shared passion for the topic. This eventually led to a brief phone call, where I was first exposed to his family's story and the inspiration behind Clint's **BigBoldBrave** coaching brand and vision. I firmly believe everyone has a valuable story to tell, and I encouraged Clint to tell his. He called me the next day and expressed his commitment to start writing the book. He also asked if I would be willing to read the manuscript. I was surprised to hear back so soon! I promised I would.

My life message is intent on a simple premise: Live in such a way as to send a motivational message that inspires everyone around you to be a servant leader and to lead with their values first. Practice these values by employing wisdom, generosity, and impeccable integrity. Together, we carry the potential to impact thousands of people, and perhaps many more. The anecdotes in this book align with that mission.

Big Bold Brave is a wonderful story of overcoming the struggles we all face—and some we hope we never have to. Clint has overcome several obstacles in his life, many of which prepared him for his greatest challenge yet. He gracefully approached a very difficult and personal topic: living out your values amid tragedy or great personal loss. Many, if not all of us, have suffered through a major setback or blow to our relationships, business, finances, or marriage. Others have had to battle against addictions, abuse, financial hardship, health issues, and many other roadblocks the highway of life can place before us.

Clint's vulnerable and honest approach in sharing how he and his wife, Amárillys, and two sons, Joel, and Liam, are walking out their destiny after the tragic death of his oldest son Gabriel is both poignant and inspiring. No one can imagine the pain of losing a child at such a young age— when they still hold such promise of a happy, healthy, and productive future—unless they have experienced it. It is a narrative no one would choose. Clint takes you on a journey through the pain, hope, love, faith, and healing process that occur when you make the courageous decision to continue to live out your values despite the cards you are dealt. He is intent on wearing his *one hat*, and you should be too! I believe this book will provoke you to make big changes, take bold actions, and bravely serve the people around you. You'll be motivated to keep living, fighting, believing, and not allow fear to dictate your life.

Although Clint and I come from different places and have backstories that are uniquely our own, we both share the belief that WE CAN live **Big, Bold, and Brave!**

Howard Behar
Retired President, Starbucks Coffee Company North America & Starbucks Coffee International
howardbehar.com

Introduction

THE WORLD HAS shifted significantly since January of 2020. For our family, this shift started on September 23, 2019. That was the day we suffered our greatest loss. Losing a child is devastating. Unless you have experienced it firsthand, no one can imagine how such a turn of events can flip your world upside down. But there are many other forms of loss that can alter your life.

I've encountered people over the years who have allowed the pain of a *death* or *significant loss* to become their identity. Families and marriages are often destroyed amid very difficult circumstances. Amárillys and I were resolute—that would not be our future. Yes, our son Gabriel was gone at the young age of seventeen. He left a gaping hole no one can fill. Our family would never be the same. But life must go on, for all of us.

The morning of our worst nightmare, I sat on the couch with Amárillys and our other two sons, Joel, and Liam. I realized if we chose to meditate on his death, how it happened, and allowed the pain of our loss to become our identity, we would each be in danger of becoming mere shadows of who we were created to be. We were severely shaken and struck down, but not destroyed. The moment required a compass that would lead us towards our futures. I told the boys and Amárillys that we would focus on honoring the way Gabriel ferociously *lived*. We would choose to view our future through a lens of *LIFE*, not death. That posture, which we established that fateful morning, is one powerful thing you'll read about in this book. It's served us well in moving forward as a family.

Later that day, while doing an interview with our Dallas NBC affiliate, our commitment to one another was given a language. I had made a statement off-camera while describing Gabriel's many passions and the impact he had on people, which the reporter then used as the segment concluded, encouraging people to, "Live like Gabriel—***Big, Bold, and Brave.***"

This quickly became our family mantra. Aside from being the title of this book, BigBoldBrave is now also my personal development coaching brand. The ideas I share in this book are not theory or regurgitated success principles gathered from other sources. They are personal—we have *lived* them! Not perfectly at times, but with consistency and intention. It's hasn't been easy, but it's been worth it!

There are legitimate emotional, mental, and physical struggles we must fight every day to pursue living **Big, Bold, and Brave**. There are the unmet expectations we had about Gabriel's destiny and pursuit of his dreams. Heck, *we* had dreams for him! We will not get to witness him standing at the altar, nervously and excitedly awaiting his beautiful bride. We will never hold his children in our arms or spoil their dinner by buying them ice cream right before bringing them home. His handsome, youthful look is frozen in time, our family photos robbed of the progression of us all aging together. And of course, there is the fear of something tragic happening to Joel, Liam, Amárillys, or me. Whether you have suffered an actual loss or not, all parents understand the battle with fear regarding our children's well-being.

So why write this book now? Time is a precious commodity. In the grand scheme of eternity, we have very little of it. Every day, we make a choice to live by our values—and so do you. You've likely suffered your own big blows. Billions of people have or will experience tremendous loss in their lifetime. The circumstances and subsequent pain come in many different forms. Yours may have been losing a business you worked years to build, getting divorced, suffering a miscarriage, or financial catastrophe. The list is endless. Unmet expectations can cast a shadow over your emotions, leading to faulty belief systems that don't serve you well. Fear and a sense of hopelessness can become heavy weights that bog you down and allow your past to steal your future. On a macro level, there are things happening in the world all around us that vie to steal our passions, dreams, imagination, and even love!

Human suffering is nothing new. It has persisted for centuries. However, there is a difference today that distinguishes current generations of people from previous ones. There has never been such a proliferation of information through so many forms of media—now literally in the palm of our hands throughout the day. Major media giants, smaller startup media companies, and individual social media influencers all volley to grab our attention, spew opinions, and sway our thoughts and actions. As a result, the sheer volume of fear, pain, confusion, and uncertainty has burgeoned in unprecedented ways, impacting virtually everyone.

Our perspective in how to respond to these issues faces a great challenge. Voices compete to kill your hope, steal your peace, and destroy your faith for a promising and better tomorrow. Dangers and risks are everywhere.

I did not write this book to deny the reality of how risky or challenging our world can be. To the contrary, I will affirm it. Life has been dangerous since the dawn of civilization. And, like it or not, humans have generally fallen into two camps in how they respond to the risks of life. The first camp slowly dies in a shroud of fear. They try to minimize their chances of failing or experiencing the pain of loving people. What's tragic is that the only way they avoid *failing* is by playing it safe and living small. They try to minimize *experiencing pain* through means of avoidance or adequately numbing it.

Some simply live in mediocrity, filled with the regret of unfulfilled dreams. They let the world around them dictate their destiny rather than dictating it themselves. Others find success in those pockets of life they feel they can control, perhaps even accumulating great wealth and influence. Yet they are haunted with a gnawing sense that there is a deep void keeping them from being truly fulfilled.

The other campers are cut from a different cloth. They understand the risky realities of life and choose to take them head on. Risks are viewed as challenges to conquer and opportunities to take. They face the same enemy of fear, but through a love and zest for *living* with purpose, they crush that fear into submission. These humans suffer pain and setbacks like each of us. But their response is very different from the first camp. Pain becomes a catalyst, propelling them forward to love the people and life around them in a more powerful, intentional way. Setbacks are viewed as temporary—as invitations to keep dreaming and courageously fighting for the future.

Listen, life is a mixed bag. There will be moments of joy AND pain. There will be times when we are strong in our faith AND when we give into fear or doubt. We may have seasons of being healthy, AND then find ourselves fighting through hell to get our health back. There will be times of prosperity AND of financial hardship. It's all part of this thing called life. Adversity is assured, but we shouldn't be stopped in our tracks by it.

Admittedly, at times I have allowed fear to creep in and stop me from pursuing what I really wanted. Aside from the quality of my marriage, the role of fatherhood, and other relationships, I found myself supremely dissatisfied. This feeling wasn't solely rooted in the tangible things I *was* doing (or in some cases, *not* doing)—it was tied to my broken philosophy in life! I was keenly aware that I was still a victim to old mindsets. I was a still member of the "fear camp" in certain areas of my life. Suffering our greatest blow would shake me from the slumber that kept me from living courageously.

I will share some of the crazy circumstances we have faced as a family and how we have made value-based decisions that brought joy and growth into our lives in every circumstance—even in tragedy. If you have suffered a great loss or setback, you CAN make a comeback. You must!

My purpose for writing this book is straightforward. **Big Bold Brave** is a direct challenge to squeeze out every ounce of juice that life has to offer. It's an invitation to a movement, not just a book full of success principles or strategies for how to grieve a loss. You'll be encouraged and inspired by our story and stories from others that I will share. You will learn how to carry hope and sustainable joy and live at peace no matter what is thrown at you. You will learn to give your pain a purpose and turn adversity into a catalyst. You will be encouraged to take risks and eat fear for breakfast! If there is an area of your life that you are not fulfilled in, this book will snap you out of complacency and commission you to do something about it! There will be thought-provoking questions and exercises at the end of each chapter to help you create the life you have longed for.

More than anything, I hope this book proves to you that love is a powerful force that can make the world around us better. We harness the ability to change people's lives, *especially* when things get tough! I believe there is an army of humans who are sick and tired of the fear, hate, negativity, and suspicion plaguing our planet, and they're ready to rise. Our family is a part of that army. We are determined to leave this world better off than we found it. No matter who you are, your backstory, or what you currently believe, I am convinced you were created to do the same.

You are unique. No one else can fill your place. The world loses if you play small or quit living.

INTRODUCTION

You only get one life on this planet. Will you hold back or leave it all out on the playing field? My hope is that when your story is told, those left in its wake will be able to say, "They lived **Big, Bold, and Brave!**"

CHAPTER 1

Our Worst Nightmare

Life has a way of punching you in the mouth. You don't have to ask for it. Whether you're old or young, rich or poor, from any racial and ethnic background—no one gets out of this world without some bumps and bruises. Many people thrive when encountering a great trial. Others seem to shrink back into the shadows, never to be heard from again. What makes them different? Is it simply that some can let the water roll off the back of the proverbial duck, while others take it all in like a sinking boat?

Why do some see opportunities in situations that appear dire, while others see no opportunity? While I do believe that certain personality types can often demonstrate a consistent resiliency in response to setbacks, I'm also convinced we all have been given an even playing field. We have it within us to be *courageous* people. Let's define "courage" according to Webster's Dictionary:

> *Courage: mental or moral strength to venture, persevere, and withstand danger, fear, or difficulty.*

Our Worst Nightmare

We were created with a nature that can respond to anything thrown at us. We can make courageous decisions that thwart any attempt of the enemy of our soul to beat us into submission. Our spirit cries out within us to choose life, not death! And that is where the rubber hits the road. There are only two choices when hardship or challenge comes. That's right, only *two*! We were hit with the reality of this truth in a way we would have never anticipated.

Imagine you're planning a trip to an exotic location for an amazing scuba diving expedition. Diving is such a unique activity. It can become addicting, instilling in people a sense of adventure that leads us to travel all over the world to explore new dive sites. However, it's important to recognize the inherent dangers and risks involved with diving, and to respect the precautions and measures that must be taken to ensure your safety underwater. Many people wisely choose to get a certification before they venture out into the water.

Open water certification teaches you the *buddy system*, meaning you will also be looking out for the safety of another diver whom you or the instructor has designated as your buddy. Because underwater communication is significantly reduced, the buddy system ensures that everyone is watching each other's backs. And before you try open water on for size, you are tested on various skills in a pool, including an assortment of situations that could be stressful during a real dive, such as losing your mask and then having to find it, don it, and clear it of water before you suffocate.

Now, imagine you're casually going about examining all the wonderfully colorful surroundings of the underwater paradise you have selected to explore. Suddenly, the unexpected happens—you bump into something you didn't see coming, causing you to lose your mask and air source! You have been thrust into using a skill you should have been trained in, but which you hoped you'd never actually need: buddy breathing.

Buddy breathing entails sharing air with a dive buddy if your air supply runs short or your equipment malfunctions while you're ascending to the surface. What if a crisis occurred and you didn't allow your buddy to share their air with you? Such a decision in crunch time could have devastating results. If you are going to choose life, then you must make a decision congruent with living, not dying—a simple decision with real-life consequences. Hold that thought.

September 24, 2019 held such a moment of truth for me. It was a Tuesday morning, and I was thrust into the very unexpected role of guiding my family in the early moments of a devastating and crushing blow. Our world had come to a halt in the form of a living nightmare.

Our seventeen-year-old son Gabriel was a private pilot. The day prior—September 23—Amárillys received a call from Gabriel's aviation mentor just after dark, around 8:00 p.m., informing us he had disappeared off the tracking system and was believed to have gone down somewhere in a remote part of the mountains on his return trip from Fayetteville, Arkansas. I walked in from running an errand to see the look of concern and hear the tremble in her voice. I immediately knew something terrible was happening. After hanging up, she caught me up to speed. Our minds began to race. Was he okay? Did he land safely somewhere with no ability to communicate? God forbid, could the worst have happened? Our minds and spirits couldn't go there, so we began to fervently pray for his safety and rescue.

Monday had begun like any other day. Life was *normal*. Gabriel had worked an early morning shift on the first day of a new job. He was working with one of his best friends, whose dad had hired him to work for his company. He was making considerably more money than his previous burger joint gig and was really excited about it!

Gabriel had also begun studying for his instrument rating certification as a pilot. He was progressing quickly. His first solo flight came at the age of sixteen, and he successfully earned his private pilot's license at seventeen. Just a few months shy of his eighteenth birthday, he was on track to realize his dream of becoming a commercial pilot. He was highly motivated, strong-willed, and didn't allow any obstacle to hold him back from attacking his goals and defeating challenges. He was *courageous*.

Earlier that morning, I'd gone out for one of my daily walks. During this season of my life, I was averaging about ten miles a day total—time used to gather my thoughts, think, pray, or just actively observe the world as it passed by. That morning, I had a brief experience that in the moment I blew off as an overactive mind, or possibly the voice of an enemy. At one point during the walk, I found myself in a deep place of thought. The world around me disappeared. Have you ever had a time when you become lost in your imagination, where everything else just disappears? It's as if you are suddenly watching a movie in your mind, but it feels real. Then, suddenly, you snap back to reality and feel as though you just had an out of body experience. This was like that.

The scene of trees, grass, and buildings disappeared into the background, and I was catapulted into a scene back at the house. I was walking around my living room with urgency and dread flooding my mind. I headed out the front door and ran across the street in search of my two neighbors, Margaret and Angela. I needed their help!

I am not conscious of the actual words I used in the conversation—nor do I recall their responses—but the situation was very clear. I asked them to take our sons, Joel and Liam (ages fourteen and nine at the time), inside with them so I could have a private conversation with Amárillys regarding something "really bad" that had happened to Gabriel. Just as suddenly as I had been thrust into this "vision," I was back on the street and once again aware of my surroundings.

As I continued walking, I realized my mind had ignored the several hundred feet of scenery I'd just passed. Since this vision was quite vivid, I walked for a bit to process its intrusive attack on my peace.

What did it mean? I quickly evaluated the strange scene and chalked it up to my imagination and the typical fearful thoughts that occur to parents over the course of their children's lives.

After all, we all have crazy thoughts regarding the welfare of our kids. And ninety-nine percent of the time they are just that: thoughts. Gabriel was 17—reason alone for us to be concerned over his whereabouts. He drove a car, had teenage friends who drove, and flew planes. His adventurous soul liked to do wild and crazy things. And so what! I would not give into fearful thoughts. And besides, the vision didn't show or tell me what had happened to him to warrant such an ominous conversation with Amárillys. I continued my walk and went about my day. I simply forgot about the vision.

Around 4 p.m. that day, he reminded me that he was flying a friend home to the University of Arkansas after she'd attended a funeral in our hometown of McKinney, Texas over the weekend. Gabriel needed the flight hours, and his friend would get back to school much quicker and avoid missing classes. He yelled, "See you later, Dad," as he rushed out the garage door and to the airport. His voice still echoes in my mind with the crushing reality that those were the last words I would ever hear him speak on this side of eternity. "See you, bud. Be careful," I yelled back.

An hour or so after receiving the news about Gabriel's plane going down, I had my first of a few frustrating calls with the local county sheriff's department that had been dispatched for search and rescue. Cell phone coverage was nonexistent where Gabriel had disappeared. We were hopeful that was why he wasn't answering our calls. The area where witnesses had reported hearing a plane in trouble was also not easy to access. The sheriff's department had no information to give us, though bits of information were already being leaked by local news stations. I couldn't help but wonder how in the world the media was aware of the situation already.

We prayed HARDER. We contacted our fiercest friends and asked them to join us in believing and praying for his safe return. We turned on music and worshipped God. We declared specific aspects of Gabriel's destiny and scriptures about divine protection. We held hope and faith that he was somehow fine. The night dragged on.

Hours went by without any definitive word from the sheriff on Gabriel's whereabouts or condition. A local news station updated their story and declared there was confirmation a small plane had crashed in the general vicinity of Prairie Grove, Arkansas.

Where was God in all of this? We were hurt, angry, and frightened, but still holding onto the belief in the goodness of God that everything would be okay. Shortly after another frustrating call with the sheriff's office, a knock sounded at our door. It was about 1:30 a.m. on Tuesday morning. I opened the door and was greeted by two fully uniformed City of McKinney police officers. This was it. My heart plummeted to an emotional depth I had never known. It was like being an actor in a familiar movie scene—only I was cast in a role I didn't want.

It turned out to be a false alarm. The officers explained they were only aware there was a crash in Arkansas. They had no new information. They'd been sent by the Washington County sheriff's department in Arkansas, which was overseeing the search and rescue. Their purpose for the early morning visit was to gather and relay our contact information to the sheriff's department, per their request. I was puzzled and angry. I'd already spoken to them three times throughout the night and had confirmed they had my correct contact information each time! The officers took down my contact information, wished me the best, and left.

I sat on the couch with Amárillys and scrolled news networks in Arkansas on my iPhone. We were still praying, still worshipping, still declaring God's scriptures that we were so certain before would protect our family against such a tragedy. After all, we had served God in full-time ministry for over nineteen years. Didn't that mean something?

Gabriel had started his return trip shortly after landing because he was excited to prepare for his second day on the new job. He had bought new boots for the job the night before. He was attending community college for some core classes and was loving it. He was plowing through the instrument rating courses required for his next certification. He had graduated from high school just a few months before, a year ahead of schedule. He had vision for his life. Everything was falling into place. We had compelling evidence that his life had many chapters left. Surely a miracle was about to take place, right?

Then the world stopped spinning. As I scrolled the local news in Fayetteville, I saw an NBC affiliate reporting a single-person fatality in a plane crash near Prairie Grove. I was sitting a few inches from Amárillys, frozen. I can say from experience: The only thing that equals the gut-wrenching news that your teenage son has tragically died is sitting in silence for several minutes trying to figure out how to tell the mother who birthed him. How do you even form words when your heart has just been crushed?

Repeating this excruciating task a few hours later with his younger brothers Joel and Liam was, given their age, arguably even harder. This wasn't supposed to be our story! I discreetly texted Amárillys' mom and my father-in-law and asked them to start heading our way from their home in Southlake. It's about a forty-minute drive to our house. We needed family *immediately*!

The strange vision from my walk on Monday morning came flooding back to my mind. Was this what that had all been about? Was that experience designed in some supernatural way to prepare me to give Amárillys the horrifying news about Gabriel? My emotions and thoughts swirled around like ingredients in a blender. Had I missed something in the message? The vision had been short and clear, but there were no specific warnings. No clues as to what the "bad" news was or why I had to deliver it. There was nothing that triggered the vision when Gabriel was leaving for the airport. Nothing felt like a warning to implore him or flat out tell him not to fly that day. I continued to sit in stunned silence searching for words, for a starting point. How in the hell do you start?

Even though we had been praying, declaring promises from scripture, and crying out to God for hours, this was the first moment I became aware that my "Dive Buddy" was sitting right there with me. He had been there the entire night, but it was in this task of having the "impossible conversation" that I sensed the presence of God's Holy Spirit. He was giving me just enough oxygen to keep from suffocating. It is no coincidence that the literal translation of Holy Spirit is *breath* or *air*. He would breathe into me and help me rise to the surface to lead our family in its most painful and devasting hour.

Courage—if that's what you'd call it in a moment such as this—rose in me just enough to speak. I reached gently for my beautiful wife's hand, looked into her tear-soaked, bloodshot eyes, and braced myself for the reaction. *"Baby, he didn't make it."* Those words still echo in my mind as I write this. It feels like a punch in the gut, every time.

I can't remember her response or the look on her face. Maybe I don't want to. My only clear memory is of us embracing, sobbing, and trembling as we held each other close. In moments like those, you can't squeeze each other tight enough to diminish the searing pain. Overpowering disbelief and confusion attack your body, soul, and spirit. We were thrust into what I now call the "shock-and-awe" faze of facing a family tragedy.

Grandpa Mike and Mima (our affectionate term for Amárillys' mom, Gladys) arrived shortly after. I shared the news with them, although it was obvious from our appearance. We desperately compared notes. Mima had been tracking the news all night. We talked through the disjointed ebb and flow of information. We tried to make sense of all the potential misinformation and apparent confusion. How was the media able to leak updates to the public but our calls to investigators couldn't yield any substantiated reports? Who was right? Maybe the news station had it all wrong? I called the sheriff again. Despite the local news report of a fatality, they would not confirm Gabriel's condition. In this small space of time, we once again held out hope and fervently prayed for a miracle, or even a resurrection!

Our miniscule strand of hope lingered until about 3:30 a.m., when we received the first call *from* the Washington County sheriff's department. A coroner had finally visited the site—a policy in place that had prevented them from telling us what everyone on-site already knew. Gabriel Anthony Hatton, aged seventeen years, nine months, and twenty-three days, was officially pronounced dead. He died from blunt force trauma on impact—seventy-seven days shy of his eighteenth birthday, carrying with him decades of hopes, dreams, and aspirations for his life.

The finality of the news was demobilizing. We sat speechless for a moment before the overwhelming emotions brought on another round of uncontrollable weeping. I remember looking over at Grandpa Mike and Mima and seeing the heaviness on their souls. They have a very special relationship with our boys and have spent a lot of time over the years with all three, especially Gabriel as he was the eldest. Deeply invested in Gabriel, they had poured love, encouragement, and time into caring for him, and they had set aside financial resources to help with college. But suddenly their dreams, desires, and hopes for Gabriel had vanished into thin air. I had great concern in the moment—especially for Mike—over whether their hearts would hold up under extreme grief. The four of us leaned on one another to survive the onslaught.

Gabriel's personality and drive were forces of nature. He was assured to fulfill an amazing destiny. In our minds, he would bring glory to God by living a long, purpose-driven life that impacted everyone around him. But it was not to be—at least not in the way we had envisioned. His journey on this side of eternity ended, and another began on the other side. Our faith assures us we will be reunited. That belief provides a measure of comfort while we wait. It doesn't change that we're left in the wake of his absence. We continue a journey without Gabriel, whether we like it or not.

We let Joel and Liam sleep in past their normal wakeup time for school. We needed that time. *I* needed that time. We gathered them into our living room and asked them to sit. With their grandparents across from them, it was obvious this was no typical morning. The presence of their Grandpa Mike in particular—a Chief of Staff for a hospital he should've been working at that morning—was the most glaring. Joel and Liam didn't ask why they were there; they just knew something was horribly wrong.

I can't accurately portray how I delivered them the news. I can only confirm it was excruciating and unnatural. The look of disbelief in their eyes is indelibly etched in my mind. Their screams and wailing were gut-wrenching. Their young hearts were broken, their innocent minds assaulted with the bluntness of death. We needed an anchor.

In that moment a wave of lucidity came to my natural mind, and a subtle peace overtook my spirit. Despite my own internal pain, I was aware we had reached a crossroad. I was only going to get one chance to set the tone for the rest of our lives. My *Dive Buddy* was there to walk me through it. The message had to be clear. If we chose to meditate on his death, how it happened, and allowed the pain of our loss to become our identity, I knew we could each be in danger of becoming mere shadows of who we were created to be. We were severely shaken and struck down, but not destroyed. The moment required a compass that would lead us towards our futures. There were only two options in how we would proceed from that day forward. I told the boys and Amárillys that we would focus on honoring the way Gabriel ferociously lived.

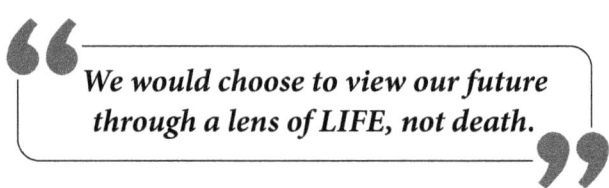

We would choose to view our future through a lens of LIFE, not death.

It was a courageous decision that would aid our grieving and healing process. A decision we would have to make again and again as the days rolled on. And if you have faced death or any forms of deep disappointment or loss, I tell you this: you have the same two choices.

Chapter 1 Reflection

Take a few minutes to reflect on the most significant loss you have experienced (loss of a loved one, divorce, broken friendship, major career setback, financial hardship, illness, etc.).

Did you intentionally take time to grieve the loss? Or did you try to tough it out, move on, and try to mask or ignore the pain?

Have you ever invited others into your pain or loss?

Are you capable of feeling joy when thinking about fond memories that occurred before the loss?

Has the sting of the loss crippled you in any area of your life? If so, describe the effect this has had on your life. For example:

- *I avoid intimacy with people because I don't want to love and get hurt again.*

- *I suppress my entrepreneurial spirit because I don't want to fail again.*

- *I have used drugs or alcohol to become my coping device and stay numb to my true emotional health.*

These are just a few questions to ask yourself that will help you evaluate how you have processed your greatest loss so far. I know from experience that allowing yourself to process pain and loss is not easy. Burying your emotions might feel easier, but acknowledging your pain and evaluating what actions you have taken (or avoided) is vital to experiencing healing and wholeness. The best is still ahead—keep reading!

Chapter 2
Life or Death

It was critical we discussed the grieving process and what it might look like for us *as a family*. The truth was that none of us could possibly predict how our emotions would manifest from one day to the next. We recognized that not every moment, and not every day, would feel successful. I told the boys that each of us was going to experience different emotions and triggers at times. If we felt sad, angry, confused, frustrated, hopeless—it was okay. Bursts of joy and laughter when fond memories entered our minds was okay too. No emotion or feeling was off limits, and there was no time limit on how long we could experience them. However, there was one strict rule: We couldn't go through any of them *alone*.

We made a pact to talk openly and honestly with each other about what we were experiencing. This would not be a one-way street from child to parent either. Amárillys and I committed to being just as open and vulnerable with the boys as we expected them to be with us. This pact has proven to be powerful. When you give each other permission to grieve in their own way with a family dynamic such as ours, you lay a foundation for healthy processes and conversations. You set an anchor point for each person to feel empowered to lean on one another. There is no fear of judgement for feeling a certain way or having a bad day. You can be honest about how you feel without fear of dragging someone else into the same emotional state.

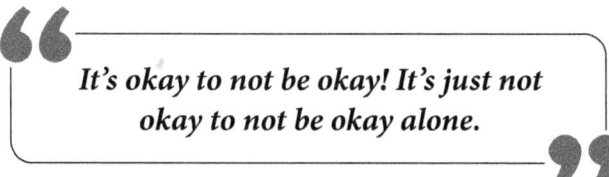

It's okay to not be okay! It's just not okay to not be okay alone.

We have not been perfect in this process. At times, we have each experienced melancholy, fatigue, lack of focus, or a lack of desire to do *anything*. It has been a war of sorts, and sometimes we have felt like we're losing a short-term battle. The trigger causing the physical or emotional reaction is not always clear at times. It can be hard to determine if you are grieving or stressed over bills, tired from a lack of sleep, or just don't have great energy on a given day. We have found it very helpful to be inquisitive and loving enough to ask each other questions if we sense one of us is suffering. We don't make assumptions about how someone is processing; we evaluate along the journey. When needed, we have incorporated help from a professional therapist. We do whatever it takes to identify, address, and restore ourselves to a healthy mental, physical, and emotional state.

There's not a human on the planet untouched by the fallout from the pandemic or one of many other great challenges our world has faced the past few years. Everyone has experienced some form of loss or death, whether literal or figurative. Your wounds may still cut deep. You may still be in the thick of loss, unmet expectations, or broken dreams. But I tell you this: Your journey isn't over. If pain has led you down dead-end roads called Regret or Hopelessness, you *can* course correct. The ancient manuscript of the Bible describes this posture:

> *I call Heaven and Earth to witness against you today, that I have set before you life and death, blessing and curse.*

> *Therefore, **choose life**, that you and your offspring may*
> *live, loving the Lord your God, obeying His voice and holding*
> *fast to Him, for He is your life and length of days.*
> *Deuteronomy 30:18-20*

There is context prior to this statement, so allow me to paraphrase. Life is short. For all of us. We will never grasp on this side of eternity why some humans live such brief lives and others long ones. No one is getting out of this human experience alive. There are risks everywhere. We are not promised breath beyond me writing or you reading this sentence. We all understand this. However, the previous biblical text unveils a secret as to how we were created. It reveals there is a tangible reality and consequence in how we respond to events in life. I believe we're given the freedom of choice by a Divine Creator. And this freedom applies to everyone without prejudice.

There is something engrained in our DNA that harnesses the ability to overcome every unfavorable and unconscionable circumstance we face. It's as real as the pain you may be feeling. It's only accessible in a relationship with your Creator. It's a choice you activate. If you don't consider yourself a person of faith, I hope my saying this doesn't frustrate you. It shouldn't. I implore you to keep reading. If I were reading your story and you considered yourself an atheist I would keep reading because *your* story matters. I hope you feel the same. Keep going.

For the record—and contrary to the popular phrase—time does NOT heal the pain of such a devastating loss. And I wouldn't have it any other way. Pain lasts because of the great love and relationship shared. What I have learned in this journey is that Jesus is greater than my pain. He is greater than we think. His ability to love, touch, heal, comfort, guide, and lead us knows no bounds. Perhaps the most telling evidence of this is that He does not demand we stay in lockstep with Him along the way. He is not offended by our anger, confusion, questions, emotional processes, warped thinking—any of our flawed human traits. He simply LOVES us through it all. He doesn't even get offended if we stop talking to Him. He is not like *us*.

Let's return to my living room on that terrible morning. Once the initial shock and tears had subsided, we paused for everyone to catch their breath. Our lives had been turned upside down and would never be the same. However, it was still *Tuesday*. Still a school day. Still a workday. That's one of the crazy things about tragedy striking—the clock continues to tick, life continues to roll on, with or without you.

One of the first things Amárillys and I had to decide was how we would finish our week. We strongly believed the boys should participate in the decision. If we were going to help carry each other through this terrible circumstance as a *family*, everyone had to have a voice.

Amárillys and I started with Joel, who at the time was a freshman in high school and played football. We allowed him to decide whether he would go to school that week, and we assured him the decision would be fully supported.

Honestly, it was tempting to make the decision for him and keep him home. On the surface, that may have been the easiest way to manage our situation and emotions. But we inherently knew it wasn't in our best interest to try and control the boys, their emotional processes, and what they felt was best for them in taking that first step back into reality. Joel didn't hesitate—not for a second. His response was, "I want to go to school. I'm going to play in the game tomorrow. I am going to play for Gabriel."

We had already discussed that the greatest way to honor Gabriel's life would be to tackle our own with the same zeal, passion, and energy he did chasing his dreams. For Joel, this meant demonstrating his skill as a football player. The next day was the homecoming game, which was a big deal. I'll admit, there was trepidation sending him to school so quickly, but it was clear he did not want to take no for an answer. I called the school and spoke with the principal. I arranged for Joel and me to meet with the principal, another staff member, and a grief counselor before sending him to his first class.

The meeting was trying. Their facial expressions were telling right as we walked into the room. I have sat with many individuals and families in the immediate aftermath of a loved one's death. I knew the look and accompanying feeling well. They had been thrust into one of those impossible situations. Their empathy for us was palpable. Yet it was also painfully obvious that they were struggling to find any words to provide a measure of comfort. Of course, there are no words.

I have learned over the years (and through personal experience) that words fall dreadfully short when someone tries to encourage you in the immediate aftermath of a situation like ours. My advice? If you engage someone who has just suffered a tremendous loss, simply say, "I love you and am here for you if you need anything." That includes by way of text or social media. That's it—no more, no less. People don't care in the moment if you went through something similar. They are not looking for magical words to lessen the pain. There is no capacity for that yet.

I sympathized with their plight and was thankful they focused on how they could support Joel in the days ahead. They were loving and kind, and we are forever grateful.

Still, I couldn't help but wonder: How many times over the course of our lives would we see the same look when people heard our story? As much as you don't want a tragedy like this to mark you, you can't wash it out or cover it up. Even though Gabriel's death did not have to become our *identity*, like it or not, it is part of our *story*. This is forever sobering.

The meeting, while brief, accomplished its purpose of ensuring that Joel knew he had support throughout the day. If things got tough, he had somewhere he could go to deal with his emotions privately. He made it through his classes and football practice.

Liam was only in fourth grade, just shy of his tenth birthday. He was certain he would rather stay home, which of course was perfectly fine with us. We had taken the first steps outside the cocoon of our living room. One step at a time, our family began to walk again—together.

The ominous task of beginning to plan a celebration service for Gabriel rapidly became our next priority. Before we could move into planning mode, there were some matters that required our attention. We had a flood of emails, texts, and voice messages from people expressing their love and condolences. I posted on social media about our need for space and privacy and asked for no expectations that we return calls or entertain visitors. We limited initial visitors to family and close friends who just wanted to hug our necks and pray with us.

People want to help in such an hour. And perhaps more urgently, they want to *show* their love. And many did. However, we also recognized we needed to comfort others. Not because we felt responsible to help others process *our* pain. Rather, it was critical for us to recognize other people were hurting and shocked by Gabriel's accident.

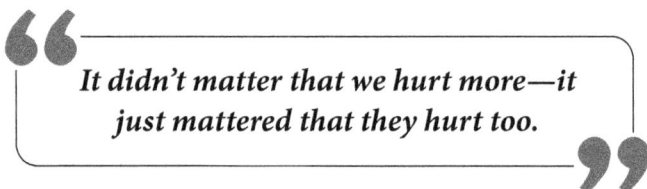

It didn't matter that we hurt more—it just mattered that they hurt too.

A couple groups of people were high priority for us. First was Avery and her mother, Mindy. Avery was Gabriel's close friend and the passenger he flew to Arkansas before his fateful return trip. Avery had been in town to attend a funeral over the weekend. Mindy asked Gabriel to fly her back home so she would not miss more school than necessary. Mindy was devastated. Avery was battling her own emotions of losing one of her best friends, plus the fact he died after dropping *her* off safely. After a few texts back and forth, Amárillys invited them over to our home to talk face to face. One of Gabriel's dearest longtime friends, Tommy, came with them. When they arrived, we embraced each other and shared a beautiful moment that entailed processing complex human emotions.

Avery and Mindy asked for forgiveness. It wasn't necessary. Who wouldn't have stopped the trip if we had known what would take place? Regardless of what had unfolded the previous night, Gabriel was doing what he loved. We expressed how grateful we were that Gabriel got her back to school safely. The only thing that could have made the tragedy more unbearable would have been loss of another life.

Avery was struggling with returning to school. She struggled with moving on, period. Amárillys emphatically expressed to her that she had a destiny, a God-given purpose to live out. We took turns encouraging her to keep living and not allow voices to convince her it was somehow her fault. Just like us, she could best honor Gabriel by living with zeal.

The same was true for Tommy. He was one of the last people to see Gabriel. He was in complete shock. They had shared countless hours together, spending the night at each other's homes, talking cars, taking pictures of cars. We have hundreds of photos of the two of them together. He was really struggling to comprehend how he could go on without Gabriel. But like us, he had to. We spoke *life*.

We hugged, cried some more, and prayed that they would receive peace and comfort. We will never forget their visit that afternoon. Our lives are forever knitted together.

Later that evening, there was another group of people we felt compelled to reach out to: the founder and members of Tango Thirty One Aero Clube. Gabriel was going into his freshman year of high school when he was introduced to his mentor, Kevin Lacey, and the club that would provide a path for him to form meaningful, lifelong relationships and fulfill his dream of flying. They were his second family, so they were ours, too. We became aware that Gabriel's crash was influencing Kevin and some of the members to consider shutting down the program.

The same program that made Gabriel's dream of becoming a licensed pilot a reality. We couldn't sit back, even in our grief, and allow fear and pain to destroy something that had been so impactful.

They had a lot to process. Kevin had lost another dear friend to a freak midair collision just a few years prior, and another pilot based out of Aero Country had recently had a close call. She is a friend and supporter of the club who crashed into a nearby home while carrying one of the club members as a passenger. Miraculously, no one in the home was injured, and they both walked away from the incident with relatively minor injuries. Ironically, Gabriel was supposed to go with them on that flight, but he had stayed behind because his buddy needed help with a project they were working on at the hangar. He would have been sitting in the rear of the aircraft and likely would have perished, as that section of the plane was destroyed on impact. Gabriel's life had been spared that day.

This was another reason the accident seemed unfathomable. Gabriel's fatal crash was a dagger in the heart of the club with the potential to be the blow that ended it. We quickly gathered the boys and headed out to the hangar to meet with Kevin, the students, and many of their parents. When we arrived, there was a larger contingent than I expected. Some of them we only knew by nicknames. One of the fun things about the culture at the T31 hangar is that Kevin eventually tags each member with a nickname. Usually there is a story or character trait behind a particular nickname. And the names stick! Gabriel's was "Skinny," a nod to his lanky figure. Others included Blue, Hammer, Professor, Ponytail, Sci-fi, and my personal favorite, Beer Money. The members are primarily high school students, so this last one requires a little explanation. Beer Money got his nickname because his parents frequently dropped off some beer for Kevin as a show of appreciation. Kevin has never told me this, but I think Beer Money may be one of his favorites!

Visiting T31 was harder than I'd anticipated. After all, Gabriel had safely left the hangar barely 24 hours prior. There was a greater force at work as we looked at the hurting faces of these precious people. We knew we had been given another platform to speak life into others. We were compelled to do so.

The purpose of our visit was simple—to comfort and encourage. We implored Kevin and the kids to take some time and strongly consider the implications of shutting down the program. Emotions were high. Gabriel was a good pilot, trained well, and was a leader in the club. His larger-than-life personality and impact could never be replaced. We told them we strongly believed that the only way to honor Gabriel and what he meant to T31 was to continue having the students pursue *their* passion for aviation. It truly seemed like the *only* decision with *life* in it. Again, a choice needed to be made. Collectively, we all chose *life*. (I will share more details about this amazing club in a later chapter.)

Our response to other people's pain doesn't make us superheroes. We found that encouraging and speaking life into others helped us navigate the early stages of shock. A strange thing about publicly suffering a great loss is that it gives you an instant platform. You don't sign up for it. Nonetheless, it's there, and the world will watch to see how you handle it. I promise you this. Giving people hope and loving them during a time of crisis does good within your soul. That's how we're geared as humans. We would soon enter a phase in the grieving process where we'd need to circle the wagons and limit how much we poured out to others; it just wasn't time for that yet.

That first twenty-four hours was a whirlwind of emotions, conversations, decisions, and considerable numbness. Wednesday arrived quickly, and the focus turned to Joel's homecoming football game. It may seem strange—if not inappropriate—to some that a football game mattered. But it did. Joel had chosen his version of life over death. He was going to perform for his brother. Without question, it was what Gabriel would have wanted.

It is hard to describe what I felt walking into the stadium. If you have ever attended a freshman game, even at a 6A school in Texas, the crowd is predictably sparse. This game was different. Word of Joel dedicating the game to his brother had spread. Some friends of Joel's (and Gabriel's) had sent texts inviting people to come, so in addition to the regular crowd, there was a little over a hundred extra fans in attendance. They had created a big sign expressing love and support for Joel, and they eagerly awaited the chance to cheer for him.

Thoughts raced through my mind as we took our seats. *How many people are here that know we lost Gabriel barely 48 hours ago? Should we even be at a game? How can I root for Joel's performance AND fight off the tears still coming unannounced in this very early stage of grieving? What if Joel doesn't play well? What effect would that have on his psyche and emotions after all the buildup with this game being dedicated to his big brother?*

Gabriel wasn't physically there to watch his brother, but his presence was felt. As the game began, the air was charged with anticipation that something special was about to happen. Joel was a playmaker. I had no concern over whether he *could* do something great—he had many times before. But the question suspended in the atmosphere was, would he do it *tonight*, under impossible conditions and the self-appointed pressure?

The coach didn't put him in right away. I don't know if the master plan was to ease him in or not. Either way, it added to my anxiety! But then, a few plays into the first offensive series, number 1 entered the game and lined up at running back. The ball was snapped, and Joel took a pitch from the quarterback on a sweep to the right. As Joel approached the corner, it was clear he was going to have a positive gain—but there were two defenders who had an angle on him. Despite his speed, outrunning them looked impossible. I expected him to cut back into the field and get a couple more yards as he was being tackled.

Then a magical moment unfolded. Joel found another gear and turned up field along the sidelines, *just* out of the two defenders' reach. The crowd roared his name as he broke away from every defender. He would not be denied! It was a forty-yard touchdown run on his first carry of the night! He even bobbled the ball a bit at the five-yard line for added dramatic effect, although the moment didn't need it.

He went on to make other big plays that night and scored a couple more touchdowns. You might be thinking, aren't touchdowns meaningless a couple days after losing our oldest child? No, they're not. Those touchdowns were little kisses from heaven and bursts of *life* needed at a very dark time for our family. I am forever grateful Joel made the courageous decision to play. And play for his brother he did!

After Joel's epic performance, we met him outside the locker room. He was surrounded by the many friends who had come to show their love for him, Gabriel, and our family. Once the crowd around him dispersed, I hugged him tight and told him how proud I was of him. His response was immediate and concise. "Dad, guys kept telling me when I made big plays what a great job I was doing. I kept telling them it wasn't me; it was my big brother." Of course, it *was* Joel who'd physically performed on the field that night. But he drew on strength from his love for his brother and a desire to provide a little injection of life into our devastating circumstances.

The rest of the week we focused on creating a celebration of life service to honor Gabriel and God. Potential for darkness to fall on each of our souls lurked around every corner. There were many tears shed that week. A few days of heavy grieving takes a toll on your body, mind, and emotional state. We struggled to eat, sleep, and think coherently. It's like sleepwalking through a mud bog thick with fog. It was a strange space to occupy. We were still in complete disbelief and wanted to wake up from this nightmare. What's stranger is that we also felt the love of God all around us stronger than ever before. It's hard to put in words, but you *can* simultaneously experience pain *and* peace, disappointment *and* hope, grief *and* joy.

I am convinced the lifeblood kept flowing for our family because of our early decision made on the couch. It was our number one priority to focus on how Gabriel lived his life, not how he died. Our resolve would be tested again and again. But fueled with the love and prayers from countless many, we would move forward one step at a time.

By now, some family had arrived from out of town, and we'd begun the unenviable task of putting together a program. There were some unexpected developments that—little did we know—would prove to be a catalyst in helping us execute our intentions. They came in forms I would have never chosen. In fact, I at first completely rejected them.

I was contacted by our local NBC News affiliate. The reporter was a kind young woman, and she was tactful and empathetic in her approach to an obviously painful and sensitive circumstance. However, she also had a job to do. She politely asked if I would be willing to go on camera and talk about Gabriel and our family's response to the tragedy. I could not imagine emotionally processing such an interview, let alone wrapping my mind around speaking without falling apart. So, I told her no. As we wrapped up the call, she respectfully took one more run at it. She explained that, due to Gabriel being such a young pilot, this was a story the news network was going to run—with or without us. She expressed she was a Christian too, and faith was part of her life. She assured me that if I was willing to do the interview, we could tell the story *our* way, including anything we wanted to say about Gabriel's life and our foundation of faith. I told her we would talk about it as a family and get back to her later that day.

After we hung up, I sat in the living room with Amárillys and my father-in-law, Santos. We were all emotionally wrecked, and an interview seemed incredibly daunting. Santos was the first to say he thought we should do it. I was surprised because he was really struggling with reconciling Gabriel was gone. Prior to the call, he had asked us if we could drive to Arkansas to where the plane went down. In disbelief, he felt he needed to see the site. (We ultimately chose not to go to Arkansas.) He felt good about us doing the interview, and his certainty shook me. But his reasoning was simple: if we were going to focus as a family on how Gabriel lived, we couldn't miss the opportunity to influence the narrative of how his story would be told to a broader audience. The story would be solely about his death, or it would honor his life. It was a wise perspective from a grandfather in tremendous pain. Amárillys and I agreed, and I called the reporter back.

Later that day, as the television crew set up in our living room, Amárillys and I braced ourselves and tried to steady our emotions. The reporter asked thoughtful questions, helping guide our responses to express in a few minutes how impactful the life of our seventeen-year-old son really was. In retrospect, it was a beautiful endeavor. Whether we recognized it or not, that interview helped us take steps during those early hours through the emotional shock and awe of tragedy. The exact words we used in most of the interview were a complete blur. But this one statement stood out and became our family mantra. At the end of the segment, the reporter finished by repeating something I had said during a part of the interview that did not air. It was that we encouraged people watching the segment to, "Live like Gabriel—**Big, Bold, and Brave.**" There was something about that phrase that was infused with *life*! As a family, we committed to this new mantra. And so, we began to attempt to do just that. Our approach to his Celebration Service would be our first public expression of this.

The Celebration Service was scheduled for the evening of September 30, exactly one week after the crash. In the wake of the initial news, there had come in many forms a massive outpouring of love and support for our family. One was an incredible gesture we'll never forget. Senior Pastor Stephen Hayes of Covenant Church—a church we've been connected with for over twenty years—was one of the first people to call. He offered the local campus facility, its resources, his staff, financial assistance, and more to aid us in celebrating Gabriel. His gesture of love was overwhelming and relieved us of enormous pressure, allowing us to focus on the service itself. We are forever grateful to him and the founders of Covenant Church, Pastors Mike and Kathy Hayes. They were also some of the first people to reach out and provide comfort, strength, and wisdom for the days ahead. Now that we had a venue, we could begin to create the service. As you read on, I want to be sensitive and clear about something. The ways we chose to honor Gabriel's life were just that: choices *we* made. The service was not done the "right" way, nor the only way. But it was the right way for us.

A few elements were non-negotiable. The first was that the service include an authentic, no-holds-barred worship experience. For us, honoring God and worshipping Him, even amid great sorrow, was paramount. We reached out to our dear friends David and Nicole Binion. They are known globally for their worship music. Amárillys and I have loved and enjoyed their gift of music for many years. However, our desire to have them be a part of this service was not for any of those reasons. It was because they were *Gabriel's* favorite worship leaders.

To our delight, they immediately accepted our invitation. The Binion's live close by, and David was in our living room just a few hours after our call to go over the music selection. The plan came together quickly and effortlessly. David even had a song he had recently written that would be a perfect fit. The worship set was going to be energetic, honor God, and express joy!

As difficult and crazy as this may sound to you, our faith tells us that Gabriel is alive again and enjoying the incredible riches of heaven. There is nothing sullen about his current residence. We understood this Celebration Service was more for us than for him. So, it was critical this portion of the program would be full of love, hope, faith, and *life*!

The next crucial decision was how to handle the absence of his remains. Due to the nature of Gabriel's death, a long and sometimes excruciatingly slow investigation by the NSTB (the federal agency that investigates all aviation accidents) was required. The coroner could not guarantee how long it would take to release his cremated remains, but we knew it would at least be several weeks. We decided against following a more traditional path of displaying a casket or urn. Instead, we would create a gallery that showcased and reflected

Gabriel's many passions and talents. By now you are very aware that aviation and becoming a pilot was a huge focus in his life. However, his interests and passions were diverse.

Among them were fascinations with photography, music, and cars. And of course, he had a wide array of friends from many different walks of life. We planned to set up displays (much like you might see in an art gallery) to share these expressions with those who came to pay their respects to his unique place in their life. There were no flowers, only displays and videos. This was important to us. Flowers are very traditional, beautiful, and are an expression of love. Our choice was driven by our desire for people to experience how Gabriel lived, what he loved, and who he loved.

The McKinney ISD Aviation program he had recently completed provided several items for the section dedicated to his love for aviation. Plane props, flight manuals, and other cool aviation-themed items set the perfect tone for the room.

We prepared dozens of his best photographs on 36"x24" gator boards and placed them throughout the foyer. There was a display in the middle of the foyer with his favorite—VERY worn—cowboy boots. There were other displays of his guitars and other meaningful personal belongings that told a more complete story of his interests.

In one corner of the foyer, a couple of large TVs played video loops. One video was of an interview our dear friends Me Ra Koh and Brian Tausend had conducted. Me Ra is a world-renowned photographer, and her husband Brian is a creative genius and expert in lighting for portraits and videos. I highly recommend checking them out! They own a studio called Fioria in Frisco, Texas. They don't just take pictures—they create an unparalleled interactive Rising Phoenix Experience. Their signature creative process results in custom wall art that reminds you every day of the powerful truth of who you are. This artwork celebrates all you've overcome and speaks to the legacy yet ahead!

We had hired them for Gabriel's senior photo shoot. And as part of a special surprise, this shoot included a personal video of Gabriel sharing with us his fond memories of Amárillys and me. That video is one of our most treasured possessions.

On display in front of the screens was a letter Amárillys had written to Gabriel when he was twelve years old. Reading that letter was one of *his* most cherished experiences. The letter was powerful and sharing it at the service was raw and intimate for her.

The setting was everything we had hoped for and more. Hundreds of teenagers were going to show up for the service. We wanted them to walk away feeling *inspired*. We wanted them to leave knowing that Gabriel had squeezed every ounce of juice out of his almost eighteen years on this planet, and that they should do the same.

Chapter 2 Reflection

I realize this chapter may stir up some raw feelings if you have lost a loved one. It's also possible you have suffered a different kind of loss that has left a trail of devastation. You may have lost your innocence, reputation, or chance at a healthy childhood. Pain from the past may be stifling your imagination or ability to be creative. There are countless others like you. I have a few questions for you to consider before we move on to the next chapter.

1. Have you ever memorialized your loss?

2. If so, did the way you memorialized it aid you in moving forward with your life?

3. Are you willing to take a fresh look at your loss and flip the script by letting it serve you in a healthier way? Having a life perspective instead of a death perspective is a game changer.

In Chapter 10, we will specifically address how you can give your pain a meaningful purpose.

Chapter 3
Perfectly Imperfect

GABRIEL WAS BORN seven weeks premature. He weighed 3lbs, 12ozs. Anyone who knew him will not be surprised by that fact. He was *always* in a hurry to experience the next thing! Gabriel had an energy about him from the time he was very little, and his motor was always running. He had a brilliant mind and excelled in school from the start. His ability to process information and articulate his thoughts was a superpower. (He used it as a weapon from time to time as well.) We were convinced that as he grew older, he could be anything he chose to be. A defense lawyer or CEO were high on the list. He loved to form arguments and defend them to death. At times, this also meant ignoring the facts. He wanted to win every argument at any cost!

He also wanted to be in control. If you knew Gabriel long enough, you discovered he had a flare for the dramatic and an occasional temper. When these traits worked in tandem, you were not sure what you were going to get. Sometimes it could be an emotional explosion. Other times he had an alternate view of reality. Case in point: When Gabriel was five, we resided in Bayou Gauche, Louisiana. We had a beautiful home and loved the neighborhood. But it was a little secluded. We'd accepted a position at a nearby church, and we didn't know anyone.

(More on that story in a later chapter.) Subsequently, it took Amárillys and I some time to get to know people and develop enough trust to have someone babysit Gabriel and Joel (who was two at the time) so we could go out on a date night.

An entire year of dateless nights flew by. We were beginning to get a little desperate for some alone time. If you're a parent of little ones, you know. Our youth worship leader, Risa, agreed to come stay with the boys one night while we went out for a few hours. Finally, just the two of us!

When we returned home, Risa had this funny grin on her face. She took us into another room, away from the boys, to tell us what had happened. Shortly after we'd left, Gabriel was sitting on the couch with Risa. He looked bummed out, so she asked him what was wrong. With a stone-cold seriousness, he turned to her and said, "They do this *all the time*."

"What do you mean?" she asked.
"They leave me alone all the time, they never take me anywhere!"

Risa had to refrain from bursting out laughing! That was Gabriel. He could be very honest, and he was loyal to family and friends to his core. But he also did not let facts get in his way at times, especially if a slight variation to the truth served his purpose. I suppose we are all like that at times. He just did it with great passion and flare.

Gabriel was a born leader, which became evident in his teenage years. He was one of the original members of T31, and he took on a leadership role his junior year. This pushed him to work hard and influence others to do the same. Of course, there was always added motivation—the sooner they got projects done to keep planes in the air, the sooner he could be flying one.

Gabriel was not a perfect leader, though. He was complex. As intense, thoughtful, or tenacious as he could be one moment, he was playful and mischievous the next! This imbalance was often tempered thanks to a little tough love and redirection from his mentor, Kevin.

Always in search of the next high-octane experience, you could not remain stationary for long if you were one of Gabriel's close friends. He loved adventure, and sometimes that required bending or breaking the rules. Again, we all can be that way at times. But Gabriel was someone who often saw rules as mere *suggestions*, or they simply didn't apply to *him*. And at times, breaking rules involved potentially dangerous behavior. Like driving a car over a hundred miles an hour!

Did I mention he had a lot of friends? Gabriel's friendship net was large and bridged a wide range of ages, races, economic backgrounds, religious views, and interests. He also had a lot of *girlfriends*. Let me clarify—he briefly dated a couple of times during high school. But by 17, he was focused on becoming a commercial pilot and was not in a hurry to find a steady relationship. He had relationships with *girls* who were close *friends*, each of whom probably thought they were his best friend. That is how he made people feel. After he passed, a few different young ladies with whom he'd never had a romantic relationship (at least that we were aware of) commented about a potential future they may have had with him. Was it because he was a little flirty? Probably. But more so, we believe, it was because he made people feel special and valued. It was a gift we all miss.

Prior to the Celebration Service, we asked people to share on social media their stories and experiences with Gabriel. The stories were astounding. As I've made clear, he wasn't perfect or a saint all the time, but none of us are! Still, the positive impact he had on people's lives during his short time on Earth was far greater and spread wider than we knew or could have imagined. Stories came in from teenagers, adult friends, and even salty older men in the aviation industry. A couple of prevailing themes and stories stood out, providing us a much clearer picture of the young man we thought we knew so well.

Gabriel loved helping people. After his death, we learned of many occasions we'd never known about. He just didn't talk or brag about them. I imagine it was because helping others came naturally, and he didn't see it as any big deal. However, the people he touched did. If you are not familiar with small, privately owned airports, there are often hangars that people live in full time. Some are amazing and quite beautiful. Life in these communities is tight. They're like small towns—*very* small towns. Everyone knows everyone. Aero Country in McKinney, Texas is one such place. Gabriel loved the people in that community.

One story involved a man who is a pillar in Aero Country. This man was elderly and had a disability. Gabriel was visiting the hangar one day in the heat of summer. The man's fans had stopped working, making the hangar smoking hot (remember, this is Texas, y'all). These aren't Walmart box fans we're talking about—they're massive fans installed high in the corners of the hangar. Upon hearing of the man's plight, Gabriel disappeared. He returned a short while later with some tools in hand. At his own peril, he climbed up into the recesses of the hangar and repaired the fans. Did I mention he was extremely handy with tools? That was Gabriel—he couldn't stand by for a minute and see a friend suffer, especially an elderly friend.

Another prevailing theme was that Gabriel loved to motivate people to try new things and take risks. Some would say he forced them! One such story involved a friend who was having a bad day. They were talking on the phone, and she expressed feeling a little down and depressed. Gabriel sprang into action. He drove straight to her house, and in the face of much resistance at first, he literally pulled her off the couch and into his car. The goal? "Let's go get you a puppy!" Off to the local rescue kennel they went. And while she did not take home a puppy, she shared this story because his energy and zest for life pulled her out of the funk she was in. Together, they had a great time.

Yet another story involved a young lady who launched a jewelry business after relentless encouragement from Gabriel. He believed in her and her talent. In his mind, she brought value to the world everyone needed to see. He was right—her jewelry is beautiful!

> *Big, Bold, Brave humans are relentless encouragers!*

Everyone needs a cheerleader like Gabriel in their life. One of our missions should be to find the gold in others around us, a topic I'll return to in a later chapter. As parents, we were blown away to discover Gabriel had this hidden life of impacting others. In the end, I think he considered what he was doing to be nothing extraordinary. Whether he understood it this way or not, he had an innate ability to find *life* in people and situations.

Again, you might think I'm implying he was an angel. Not at all. I had a dream one night, in which I was compelled to investigate the contents of his backpack. As I searched, I found an empty gold-colored foil wrapper that had the name of a vaping product on it. When I awoke the next morning, I went into his closet and began a real search. Sure enough, I reached into the exact place in the backpack I had looked in the dream and found an empty gold foil wrapper and a vape pipe. Busted! We had the obvious conversation about taking care of his body, the dangers of vaping, and that hiding things from us was futile! I'd like to say he quit vaping that day, but it was probably sometime after that.

On another occasion, Amárillys dreamt about a particular girl driving in a white SUV. Amárillys sensed the dream was showing her that Gabriel was dating someone behind our back. When confronted, he fessed up. We worked through it. He learned from experience that his parents seemed to have a secret source that provided us with insider information when he was making poor decisions. He never got away with anything for too long. We shared many laughs about it with him, and we found out later that he'd relayed private information to his younger brother, Joel: Stay out of trouble!

Gabriel had a fire inside him that didn't always create a warm, cozy environment. You could get burned by its intensity. He could be dramatic and have epic temper tantrums, which started at a very young age. Fortunately for us, it didn't happen often. But on occasion, when he didn't get his way about something, the show would begin. The world was against him—specifically *we* were against him. He would roll around, scream at the top of his lungs, and accuse us of horrible parenting. When he was still little, we sometimes let him roll around on the floor until he was exhausted. Once, we even shot a video of a tantrum. After he'd calmed down, we asked if he wanted to see what he looked like. Oddly enough, he never wanted to watch the video! His tantrums must've sounded like murder scenes to our neighbors, and I was always amazed no SWAT teams ever showed up.

Once he hit his early teens, this phenomenon was rare but could still surface. One night, we experienced an emotional *firenado*. If you've never heard this term, picture a fire in the form of a tornado. They're uncommon, only occurring when turbulent air rapidly rises from the site of a fire, thus causing flames to act like a tornado. Point is, they are downright terrifying. Anyway, one evening Gabriel was upset with us. I don't remember the topic or source of friction. When he did have a blow up, the topic often did not match his reaction, though it probably had something to do with us not allowing him to do something that EVERY other parent on Earth allows *their* kid to do. If you know, you know.

The conversation started in the kitchen. Things quickly escalated as he got into a shouting match with Amárillys. I stood close by, trying to calm him down by yelling over him. Of course, this is something you never see professional hostage negotiators do because it doesn't work! As I yelled, he got angrier. At one point, he got nose-to-nose with her and was screaming in her face. It looked like contact might accidentally occur, so I stepped in and physically separated them. With his attention now turned to me, a fight ensued. I did my best to wrestle him to the ground and pin him. I didn't want either of us to regret throwing a punch. When I let him go, he stormed off to his room. I followed him. And while no punches were thrown, the fight did end with harsh words. He said something he knew would cut deep, and I responded in kind. I instantly regretted it. It was not one of my finer moments. I was ashamed to have not had better self-control in the heat of the moment.

Things eventually calmed down. The next day, Amárillys and I talked about how we would revisit the situation with him. It was completely unacceptable to treat his mom that way. We could not just let it go. We knew we needed a different strategy—taking his phone, car, or privileges away would not help. Punishment was not the goal. Rather, we wished to maintain a connection with him and use this as a teachable moment to influence his future behavior. It would start with me apologizing for my harsh response. I let him know what he said had hurt me, but I was without excuse in returning a hurtful response.

Next, I took him out to dinner for sushi, one of his favorite cuisines. During dinner we talked about what had occurred in our kitchen. I explained why we would never be okay with that kind of behavior towards his mother. He needed to understand that if he could act that way with Amárillys, whom he had a great relationship with and loved deeply, he could treat another woman even worse. He needed to learn *now* how to treat a future girlfriend or wife. Abusive behavior was inexcusable. It's important to note: Gabriel was not an abuser. But that night, he acted in an abusive manner.

Prior to getting inner healing, I had to overcome my own tendencies in dealing with conflict. I have a few past relationships in which, I regret to say, I acted abusively. Amárillys is fortunate to have never met my old self. I wanted better for Gabriel and any woman he might eventually date or marry. I implored him to act with nobler motives and told him his display of anger was not his identity. He received the conversation well, like an adult. As we got in the car to leave, I told him the second part of our plan.

The following week, he would take his mom out on a date. I trained him in the basics: how to politely ask her out, open doors for her, and seat her first at the restaurant. I gave him money to pay for the meal. They had a wonderful time together, and the relational bridge was easily mended. He never repeated that kind of behavior.

Gabriel was a funny, kind, brilliant, friendly young man. As I said, he had a special soft spot for the elderly. We loved that about him. He graduated a year early from high school, worked hard at his jobs, became a licensed pilot, taught himself to play the guitar, was an amazing photographer, and left a lot of people's lives better than they were before they'd met him. As extraordinary as he was at seventeen, he could still be a typical, immature teenager who thought he was smarter than his parents. He made some bad decisions.

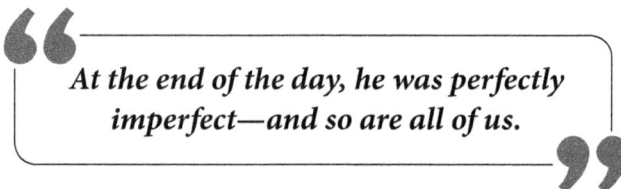

At the end of the day, he was perfectly imperfect—and so are all of us.

I think you'll agree that none of us are perfect. However, some humans have a lifelong struggle to *achieve* perfection. They're never happy with themselves or their accomplishments. They will never feel good enough to deserve love, affection, accolades, intimate relationships, etc. They will never accomplish enough because there is always more, or they could have done it *better*. It's sad. Perfection is a terrible goal to strive for. I'll prove it to you with a definition of "perfect" from Oxford Languages:

Noun
1. Having all the required or desirable elements, qualities, or characteristics—as good as it is possible to be.
2. absolute; complete.

Verb
make (something) completely free from faults or defects, or as close to such a condition as possible.

I have eaten the perfect Belgian waffle and picked out the perfect tie for a special occasion, but I don't know any perfect people. Do you?

Only One has ever walked the planet, and that was long ago. If you are waiting until you are perfect to live your best life, it will never materialize. If you want to have an impact on this planet, I have great news for you: perfection is not required! In reading the Bible, you discover the scriptures are full of perfectly imperfect people God used to do incredible things. Modern history has seen some amazingly imperfect people accomplish extraordinary feats: Martin Luther King Jr., Mother Theresa, Steve Jobs, Walt Disney, and Winston Churchill to name a few. Each of these humans made significant, enduring contributions to our world. Each had their flaws. They are not known for their flaws; they are remembered for their impact.

> *My hope is that your imperfections don't cause you to play small. No one wins if you do.*

There is a hole in the world shaped in your image. You must rise to the occasion and fill it with your unique strands of DNA. I'm not talking about becoming famous or wealthy, curing cancer, or building a massive company that employs thousands. Those are all things you may *do*, but they do not define *you*. Being famous, wealthy, or doing something BIG has been exalted in our culture as the epitome of success and influence. It shouldn't be. I *am* talking about being the biggest, greatest, healthiest version of *you*. Imperfections and all. If you are willing to commit to living **Big, Bold, and Brave** the rest of your life, I invite you to keep reading. All imperfect humans are welcome!

Chapter 3 Reflection

Do you strive to be a perfectionist? Write out in detail why or why not.

In your opinion, is perfection a measurable and obtainable goal? If yes, how will you know when you have reached it?

What personal characteristics or traits do you consider to be your most valuable?

What personal characteristics or traits do you consider to be your weakest?

Now, in what ways could you increase the value of your strengths to greater impact the world?

There is an enormous amount of data suggesting we are far more effective humans when we focus our energy on improving our strengths instead of trying to become stronger in areas of weakness. For clarity, I am specifically referring to our God-given abilities and the uniqueness of our personality, including our creative and intellectual thought processes. Moral weakness is an area we should all desire to address and improve.

CHAPTER 4
YOUR LIFE MESSAGE

THE DAY OF the celebration service came quickly. Its scope had grown significantly throughout the week. An unexpected addition to honoring Gabriel took shape quickly with the coordination of Gabriel's aviation mentor, Kevin Lacey. Kevin had been in communication with a few local pilots—including a couple of close friends—to kick the celebration service off with a flyover. Once the ball started rolling, Kevin began getting calls from pilots all over the Dallas Metroplex. What started as a small cluster of a few friends turned into a complex plan to coordinate over twenty aircraft over the airspace directly above the church. Pilots either knew Gabriel or had heard his story and wanted to participate.

When we arrived at the church, hundreds of people already filled the parking lot. The love and support were remarkable. One of the first groups we encountered consisted of some football coaches from McKinney Boyd High School. They had organized a large group of players dressed in their bright red home game jerseys. This was only a few days after that epic homecoming game. Seeing them was very emotional.

Old friends from out of state had come all the way just to be with us in this moment. One couple even drove all day from Pennsylvania and had to return that night after the service! There were school administrators, students, teachers, Tango Thirty One Aero Club members, and several close-knit neighbors we are blessed to have on our street. We were overwhelmed by the outpouring of love and support. We also couldn't help but notice many people who had not been together in the same room for many years. It was breathtaking and astounding. We sensed more was going on than we planned for or even could have imagined. The sanctuary quickly filled past standing room only, and an overflow area was set up in two different rooms. The estimated attendance was over a thousand people.

After greeting extended family in a private room, it was almost time to start. My mind raced, my heart pounded, and it took everything in me to hold it together. Everyone gathered in the parking lot and patiently awaited the flyover. During the wait, I conducted another interview with a local Fox News reporter. He had requested my permission to be on site, interview me about the service, and record some footage. His dad was a pastor, and he wanted to be part of telling Gabriel's story and our handling of the tragedy.

The flyover's constant flow of aircraft was impressive. In the days that followed, we talked to people in the community who had not attended the service but had watched all the planes doing their pattern. The reaction was the same each time: They thought it looked like an air show, or pilots practicing for an upcoming event. The variety of planes and the different sounds each made was captivating. There were over twenty aircraft in all, though the final number was hard to pin because some joined in late and were not part of the official role of approved participants. Kevin Lacey had gone to great lengths to organize and plan a safe flyover, and he had to turn away some pilots who didn't have enough flight experience to be in such close airspace with so many aircraft. Among the aircraft were a variety of Cessnas, four models of RVs, four Piper Cherokees, two Beechcraft

Bonanzas, a Twin Comanche, a Velocity, and a Bellanca Viking. It was remarkable.

The planes performed two full patterns. As the last group approached, we steadied our hearts for a very special moment. The flyover would end with an aerial salute called the *missing man*. The missing man formation is an aerial salute performed as part of a fly-past of aircraft at a funeral or memorial event, typically in memory of a fallen pilot, a well-known military service member or veteran, or a well-known political figure. Execution varies, but in this case a single aircraft would break formation and fly away from the formation to symbolize a departure from this life.

Part of what made the scene so special was the Cessna 150 used for the breakaway. Nicknamed 35Ugly, it was Gabriel's favorite to fly. What really broke us was that it was piloted and co-piloted by two of his closest friends and fly buddies, Alex Coats and Kevin Butler (nicknamed Blue and Hammer, respectively). They had shared many adventures with Gabriel. Just two months prior to Gabriel's crash, they had flown a caravan of planes with some other T31 members to the biggest air show of its kind in the world—AirVenture Oshkosh in Oshkosh, Wisconsin. As they flew directly above the site of the celebration service, Alex broke formation and flew off west into a spectacular sunset.

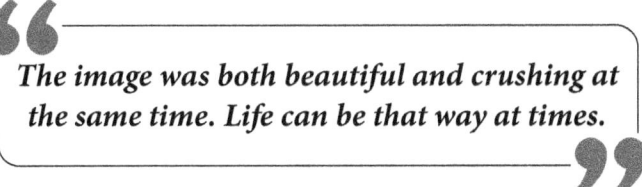

> *The image was both beautiful and crushing at the same time. Life can be that way at times.*

It was time to worship, so the crowd then made their way back inside the building. After a quick greeting by the officiant—Gabriel's godfather and our long-time mentor, Pastor Gordon Banks—the Binion's and their team began to play. I recognize as you read this you may have an image of church worship in your mind based on your personal experience. There are many expressions, styles, and sounds, just as there are in popular music. All styles are beautiful and meaningful to the individual congregation. Some like their worship soft, some loud. Some enjoy celebratory dancing, while others prefer more subdued and introspective proceedings. This celebration was about *life*. For us, that meant energetic music (some might say *loud*) espousing joyful declarations of the goodness of God.

We gave God everything we had in us. We honored Him, grateful for the life we had shared with Gabriel. We sang, danced, raised our hands, and wept. God's presence was tangible. We were aware that some may have been puzzled by our exuberance given the terrible circumstances, and that was okay. We worshipped for God and for us. We would later hear reports from different people in the service about how thick the atmosphere *felt*, especially from those who do not attend church or who have never worshipped in that way. They couldn't put their finger on what they were experiencing—they just knew that it was palpable, and it made them feel good.

I believe what they experienced that night was genuine love. Love that God had for our family and everyone in the room, and love that we had for God. It was the perfect launching pad for what would come next.

A parade of a few close friends and family members were set with the unenvious task of saying (in just a few minutes) what Gabriel had meant to them. I'm sure many of you reading this have had a similar experience. What should realistically merit days—if not weeks—must be done in an hour or two. It is an impossible task that leaves you feeling like you didn't do enough to honor your loved one. And while we could have gone on for several hours, the celebration was wonderful and powerful. Many stories were told, most of which invoked sincere joy and laughter. It became clear that we were celebrating a complex, perfectly imperfect young man.

His strengths and weaknesses, his talents and shortcomings, the way he touched people and on occasion annoyed the fire out of them—all were on display in these stories! And isn't that a reflection of our humanity? We are each uniquely and wonderfully made just the way we are. There is no one on this planet like *you*. You carry a life force and value that only you can bring.

One obvious takeaway from Gabriel's life was his unapologetic, even brash at times, way of attacking life and all it had to offer. He consistently brought his genuine self into the mix. He was a loyal son, brother, grandson, nephew, cousin, and friend. He was a pilot, photographer, guitar player, and car enthusiast. He was adventurous, humorous, dramatic, and much more. He left a huge void in our hearts and a major footprint on the lives of those who knew him. He embraced challenges and refused to play small—and you should, too!

Towards the end of the night, it was time for Amárillys and I to step up to the mic. It's impossible to describe the thoughts and emotions that flowed through us. We were challenged with fear and concern that we could keep our emotions steady. Many parents choose not to speak in a similar setting, which is both understandable and appropriate for some. But for us, we felt there was a mission in honoring Gabriel. Our journey to live the rest of our lives **Big, Bold, and Brave** and to carry his legacy forward was going to be put on public display once again. As we looked out into the standing-room-only crowd, the weight of the moment became even heavier.

It was impossible not to notice the incredible diversity of people who had come to show love and support for our family. Most astounding was the number of teenagers. Many of them were clustered together in one large group. Staring into their eyes, I saw silent, deafening cries to make sense of it all. They were in pain. The thin veil between life and death had become far too real. They missed their friend.

As grieving parents, we didn't owe anyone anything, and no one demanded anything of us. But we were very aware that—one way or another—our words would have an impact. Our emotions at this point were vulnerable and raw. The microphones felt heavy in our palms. Once again, a choice had to be made.

As Amárillys raised her mic, she transformed from a weeping, grieving mother trying to hold it together into a roaring lion. With great passion, energy, and strength, she figuratively took her hands and cupped the chin of every face stooped in sorrow. She lifted them up to look her in the eyes, her voice demanding full attention. I will never forget that moment. Even now I'm getting teary-eyed writing about it. With great care, love, and remarkable grace, she shaped how these young people should respond to losing their friend. She ferociously challenged them to crush any fear of death or purposelessness they may be feeling, and to instead turn to God and have faith and hope for a bright future. It was powerful. I witnessed an immediate change in the atmosphere and countenance of many of the kids and other attendees.

Then my turn came. I had prepared some notes to stay on track and avoid falling apart. I had written down a couple of personal stories. My favorite was admittedly a little self-serving. As I said before, Gabriel was *very* mechanically inclined. When it came to cars, bikes, or anything mechanical, he *never* needed my help. Ever. Until one day.

He was planning to paint the brake calipers on his car. He had parked the car in our garage, jacked it up, and was about to take the wheels off. But he came in a short while later, visibly frustrated. He'd been attempting to remove the first wheel, but the lug nuts were so tight, he couldn't get them to budge.

I went out to see if I could help. I placed the wrench over the first lug nut and prepared to use all my force to try and loosen the bolt. To my surprise—and even more, his—I turned it easily. His jaw dropped—the look of disbelief was unforgettable. I effortlessly loosened all five and quietly handed him the wrench. No words, just a matter-of-fact silent gesture of "here you go" while on the inside I laughed hysterically. I left him in the garage and went inside to humbly tell my wife what just happened. Okay, not so humbly! But hey, this was a historical moment for me!

To my delight, he came back inside a few minutes later with a sheepish look on his face. He told me he couldn't budge the bolts on *any* of the wheels. "Can you help me again?" he asked in a defeated tone. "Sure," I said, still masking the great pleasure I felt inside. He watched as I removed the bolts on the three remaining wheels, again with minimal effort. He just shook his head and said "thanks." I may or may not have made a comment about *dad strength* before heading back inside. I don't recall ever having another conversation with him about it. It makes me giggle and smile whenever I think of it. I told a couple more stories about my amazing son and urged the kids to honor his life in the only way they really could: by living theirs with great passion and intention!

Experiencing death firsthand affects you like nothing else can. The vivid awareness of the frailty and brevity of life touches us all. And when it comes to our loved ones, no one lives long enough. I only knew one of my grandparents growing up as a child. My Grandma Ruby lived to the ripe old age of 95. It still wasn't long enough. The truth is, even though it can be easier to accept when someone passes after a long and productive life instead of one cut short, death is an experience we always would rather do without.

At some point, we're all brushed with the death of a loved one. And we'll all eventually die. Sadly, many are crippled by the great loss or disappointments of life. These people quit living before their physical bodies have. This is both tragic and unnecessary.

A brush with death can bury us under a weight of hopelessness, or it can be a catalyst that motivates us to live life to the fullest. Losing my son has made me think about dying. It brought me to a conclusion:

> *Do not fear you will die; be terrified you quit living before you do.*

Do *you* think about dying? Maintaining a self-awareness that we only have a short number of days on this side of eternity can be a healthy thing. The awareness that we are not guaranteed another day can drive you to be more present with the ones you love. It can lead us to take an extra day off or leave work early, put down our smartphone and be present with our spouse or kids, have more family dinners, or even change our career to live by a different set of values. It can awaken us from sleepwalking through life, wasting day, after day, after day.

Gabriel's message on Earth spoke volumes to people more than we ever imagined. If I were to start making t-shirts with his life message, one would be this ... *What's Next*?

I hope your life message speaks volumes too. We each send life messages all the time, whether we are conscious of it or choose to embrace it. The people around us receive those messages and are supremely influenced by them. I believe how we interact with people along our journey ultimately determines the message we leave behind. It seals our legacy.

Let's get practical and look at the characteristics of maintaining a *life* perspective. It doesn't require massive acts of heroism. In fact, the message you send to others about who you really are is contained in what I'm about to outline. Doing so requires employing these powerful character traits that we all have access to. Each send a message to those we encounter along our journey. Your legacy will—or won't—reflect these when people remember you.

Some good news in advance: If you detect a deficiency in any of these traits, be encouraged! You can grow in them!

Love: Love is the greatest source and motivating factor for having a *life* perspective in any situation.

The English word "love" has become a lot like the Hawaiian word "aloha." It can have various applications. Many would agree the word has become so watered down that it carries little weight anymore, or that it's too ambiguous. There is something called the Law of First Mention, essentially meaning the first time a thing is mentioned or recorded in human history. The love I am describing here is from the ancient texts of biblical scripture, written thousands of years ago.

Love in its purest form is void of all selfishness. Love is unbiased. It has no expiration date and is limitless in supply. Love is a gift, not a possession. It can only be given, not taken. It is the only force on the planet that harnesses the ability to turn even the direst circumstances around. It can turn enemies into allies in the blink of an eye. Every wicked, disgusting, and violent act of humanity—whether through an individual, group, organization, or government—is triggered by the absence of love.

The traits I will list next are all byproducts of love. They are each powerful and will serve you well if you consistently employ them.

Joy: Joy is a potential state of mind and spirit. Joy is also personal. It is not dependent on others or circumstances. Joy can be experienced simultaneously with happiness but is altogether *different* in substance. Happiness is momentary and situational. It is a temporary sentiment fluid with the ebbs and flows of life. Joy can be sustained over a lifetime, even during moments void of happiness.

Peace: Peace is a multifaceted, tangible substance that can be acquired in any circumstance or decision you encounter in life. I will cover peace in more detail in Chapter Six.

Patience: Patience is probably the most elusive trait for most humans—especially those living in large cities and parts of the world with high levels of stress. Patience is elusive for me at times! Patience does not demand its way. Patience is willing to withhold judgement until all the facts are gathered. It doesn't require other humans to change on a subscribed timeline. Patience is connection oriented, not punishment driven. It is long-suffering and, with wisdom, accommodating. Patience thinks in terms of destiny, not destination.

Kindness: An action of humility. A humble human doesn't allow pride or arrogance to guide their behavior. Kindness is expressed through being friendly and considerate of the uniqueness of others. Kindness is not hindered by gender, age, race, economic status, religious stance, political slant, sexuality, cultural difference, or the like. A kind, soft response can turn away wrath. This world needs an infusion of kind humans.

Generosity: A trait that seeks to be a blessing to those around us. A generous soul freely and judiciously gives their time, talent, and resources. A generous mindset says there is always enough to go around. Poverty mentalities hoard—for them, there is never enough. Some of the most generous people on the planet might be financially poor, and some of the most uncharitable can be wealthy. A generous person carefully stewards their resources.

Faithfulness: A faithful person does the right thing for the right reason, even when no one is there to witness it. They are loyal and dedicated to a relationship, cause, or organization they align with. They overflow with integrity and will honor their end of the deal no matter the sacrifice. A faithful person's word is their bond.

Gentleness: This trait can be mislabeled as weakness. Gentleness is anything but weak. It's true quality is in its calm, confident strength. It handles conflict with a thoughtful, kind response, not an emotionally charged reaction. This temperament is conducive to being a deep thinker. Gentleness does not demand attention. It avoids displaying boisterous or rambunctious behavior.

Self-control: Those who exercise this trait are consistently powerful. They take full responsibility for their thought patterns, emotions, habits, financial status, and how they react to the events of life. They take steps to maintain the health of their body, soul, and spirit. They embrace the value of input from those they are close to without losing themselves or giving away their power. They recognize that life is full of choices and opportunities.

I should point out here once again that none of us perfectly execute these character traits. We all fall short at times. The goal here is not perfection, it is intentionally portraying a value of these traits and demonstrating them consistently. When I'm not doing that, I clean up my mess by acknowledging that the message I sent was the wrong one. I ask for forgiveness and choose to adjust my behavior to align with these traits and values. My consequential behavior reveals the life message I am committed to.

You will find there is a transcendent truth in our world. What you are willing to release, you will receive more of in return. In fact, you cannot receive the fullness of something you're not willing to give away. This truth influences your life message. Here are some examples:

When I release love, I receive more love in return.

When I release peace, I receive more peace.

When I release joy, I receive the ability to sustain my joy.

When I release patience, I receive more patience.

When I release kindness, I receive kindness in return.

When I release generosity, I receive an increased ability to be generous.

When I release faithfulness, I receive faithful people in my life.

When I release gentleness, I receive a gentle response.

When I release self-control, I receive more power to remain controlled.

Living a **Big, Bold, Brave** life requires being intentional about the message I am sending to the world. I must change the narrative if it's not leaving the legacy I want. Do whatever it takes to develop these traits. Here are a few ways:

- Read a book about how to grow in an area of your life.

- Observe and learn from people that have proven to master a trait.

- Listen to a podcast on the subject.

- Find a workshop to attend.

- Stay away from the mall at Christmas (kidding).

I heard a story once, though I can't remember where or who from. It went like this:

> *One day in 1888, a wealthy and successful man was reading what was supposed to be his brother's obituary in a French newspaper. As he read, he realized the editor had confused the two brothers and had written an obituary for him instead. The headline proclaimed, "The merchant of death is dead," and the obituary then described a man who had gained his wealth by helping people kill one another. Not surprisingly, he was deeply troubled by this glimpse of what his legacy might have been had he actually died that day. It is believed that this incident was pivotal in motivating him to leave nearly his entire fortune following his actual death eight years later. This money funded awards each year for those whose work most benefitted humanity. This*

is the true story of Alfred Nobel, the inventor of dynamite and the founder of the Nobel Prize.

The message in this story is simple—what will you be remembered for? You can influence your storyline. Gabriel, flaws and all, is remembered by most as a kind, funny, ambitious, intelligent, energetic human who would fight to the death for his family and friends and who loved to serve people. That's pretty good in my book. How will YOU be remembered? If you don't like the answer, it's never too late to change it.

Chapter 4 Reflection

Describe in your own words why you feel it's important to leave a life message behind that you can be proud of?

If leaving a positive life message behind is not important to you, describe your reason for feeling that way.

A great litmus test to determine how you will be remembered is to measure how consistently you live out the characteristics emphasized in this chapter. On a scale of 1-10, rate how well you represent the following as they were described:

Love

Joy

Peace

Patience

Kindness

Generosity

Faithfulness

Gentleness

Self-control

Write a eulogy—yes, a eulogy! Use language that expresses what you would want people to say about you when your time on Earth is up. This may sound strange, but if you can't express how you want to be remembered, you lack direction for creating your life message.

CHAPTER 5
THE FEDEX GUY

Oんe of the painfully slow realities of our son dying in a plane crash was knowing that the NTSB investigation would take a long time. It was estimated to last between eighteen and twenty-four months before its conclusion and the final report would be issued. This timeline is typical for this type of airplane crash. The other issue was the delay in the coroner releasing his body. I had been on the phone with the coroner a couple of times over the course of the first two weeks and could not get a firm date on when they would conclude their autopsy. Due to the violent nature of the crash, our only option was for Gabriel's remains to be cremated.

We were still in the early "shock and awe" stage. I call it that because wrapping our minds around such a sudden tragedy was still impossible. We had not yet felt the full weight of an entire calendar year without him. As anyone who has lost a loved one knows, it's the parade of birthdays, holidays, school milestones, and other special occasions that routinely jolt you into dealing with the emotional void left by their absence.

All things considered, I was doing well. And although I had shed many tears and the pain was still raw and fresh, I had not experienced mental or emotional despair or depression. My faith was intact, and my eternal perspective had kept my heart light. But it was about to be put to an excruciating test.

One Wednesday morning, Amárillys and I were going about our business, doing our best to move forward in what was slowly becoming our new normal without Gabriel. The doorbell rang and our dog Bailey went nuts, ferociously barking as she customarily does at any intruder. She is, admittedly, a poorly trained dog. She knows two tricks: sit, and shake. That's it.

Given that we are doing our part to keep the Amazon machine and other fledgling online retailers churning by having packages delivered almost daily, there was nothing unique about this encounter. I looked through our security glass and saw the FedEx delivery guy. Whew, turns out we were safe after all, and Bailey could chill out!

I stepped out and shut the door behind me to sign for the package and keep Bailey from mauling the guy. The delivery driver handed me the device to register my signature. A millisecond before I touched the stylus to the screen, I glanced at the package in his hands. That's when I saw it: In bold red letters, the words *cremated remains* were written on the side. The box had one of those bright orange *biohazard* stickers on it. I was stunned. To say the moment was surreal is a gross understatement. I looked in the driver's eyes to discern whether he had any clue what he was asking me to sign for. But he was just doing his job. He probably hadn't even looked at the box when he grabbed it out of the truck. The scene had an eerily morbid feel to it. I returned my attention to the device, signed, said thank you, and stepped back inside with the box in hand.

As I made my way to the kitchen, Amárillys approached to see what the package was. I don't recall what we said to each other or if we exchanged any words at all. Together, we cut open the box and extracted the container inside that held the ashes of our seventeen-year-old boy. My heart plummeted. Even writing this, my gut sinks.

Are you kidding me? I thought. We began to cry the heaving kind of tears where you can't catch your breath, your eyes instantly puff up, and snot comes out of your nose. We could only stand there and hold each other. There is no way to console someone during such a moment. There is nothing that prepares or trains you how to respond. You simply weep, *intensely.*

Once we'd gained a semblance of composure, Amárillys went off into our bedroom, while I remained in the kitchen staring at the container. The weather in my soul suddenly shifted. Dark clouds of an emotional descent began to roll in. The weight of the darkness was heavy, attempting to engulf me. I could tangibly feel the storm taking over. This was not grief or a temporary emotional reaction—the enemy of my soul wanted to pummel me into a state of despair and depression. It desired to cripple my faith and throw me overboard into a sea of deep resentment and bitterness, with cement blocks chained to my feet to keep me submerged. As hopelessness began to trailblaze a new pathway in my brain, I had a sudden lucid thought.

I can't describe exactly how I sensed it, but I recognized I'd been given a brief window to stop the onslaught. I mustered enough fortitude to lift my arms, much like I had when we were worshipping to songs at Gabriel's Celebration Service. I softly began to say out loud—honestly, mutter at first—things I was grateful for.

Gratitude felt like an unwelcome response to the situation. Despite this, I continued to express gratefulness. I thanked God that I was given the opportunity to be Gabriel's dad. I thanked Him for some of the memories that were now flickering through my mind. I thanked Him for letting Gabriel accomplish his dream of becoming a pilot. My voice grew stronger and clearer. I could still sense the black storm clouds that had descended just a minute before, but as I continued to express gratefulness towards God, another *suddenly* occurred.

I literally *felt* the heavy blanket covering me torn off. Gratitude welcomed a *Peace* that instantly overcame chaos. I could breathe again, and my emotions settled. The pain was still there, but the enemies of my soul named despair, hopelessness, anger, depression, resentment, and bitterness were instantly defeated. They were outnumbered by one Incredible Force. It was a profound experience, one I will never be able to forget or dismiss. I had felt peace before, but never so vividly.

There is an account in the scriptures of an event Jesus and his disciples went through that mirrors my experience:

> *"On that day, when evening had come, he said to them, 'Let us go across to the other side.' And leaving the crowd, they took him with them in the boat, just as he was. And other boats were with him. And a great windstorm arose, and the waves were breaking into the boat, so that the boat was already filling. But he was in the stern, asleep on the cushion. And they woke him and said to him, 'Teacher, do you not care that we are perishing?' And he awoke and rebuked the wind and said to the sea, 'Peace! Be still!'* **And the wind ceased, and there was a great calm.*"***
> Mark 4:35-39 ESV

Where the disciples only saw dire circumstances, Jesus continued with his nap. While they could only see through a lens of death, Jesus snoozed—secure He was the embodiment of life. While the physical realities of a dangerous storm tossed their boats around and gripped the sailors with fear and hopelessness, He was perfectly calm. He didn't just command peace—He *was* Peace!

- Do you sometimes struggle with keeping your peace? There is much that can make peace elusive.

- Is the stress and pressure of your job or business making it hard for you to sleep through the night? Or is it fear that something will happen to you or your children?

- Do you fear you're going to die prematurely?

- Do you require faulty coping mechanisms like drugs, alcohol, sex, working long hours, or extreme exercise, all of which only temporarily mimic a calming peace?

- Does your mind race or your blood pressure rise when faced with a difficult decision?

- Do you tend to side towards a negative view of life rather than hoping for a positive outcome?

- Have you suffered great loss like ours? Have you been suffocating under the weight of grief for years?

You CAN learn to find peace in any situation. But you likely can't do it without God. Admittedly, many Christians live their entire lives without resting in *this* Peace. I *am* compelled to tell you, however, that Divine Peace countered an assault on my mind and emotions. Divine Peace kept the pain of loss from poisoning my soul and potentially causing me to withdraw from my wife, boys, friends, and responsibilities. Please indulge me with one more scripture:

> *"Don't be pulled in different directions or worried about a thing. Be saturated in prayer throughout each day, offering your faith-filled requests before God with overflowing* **gratitude***. Tell him every detail of your life,* **then God's wonderful peace** *that transcends human understanding will guard your heart and mind through Jesus Christ."*
> *Philippians 4:6-7 TPT*

Don't let the phrase "saturated in prayer" confuse you. The prayer described here simply implies *talking* to God. It's not a long chant. There are no magical words you need to know or memorize. It's an ongoing conversation. Do you have a great friend you talk to everyday? It's like that. I am hoping what really strikes you is this:

> *Gratitude is an intentional action that invites, among other things, a supernatural force called Peace. This Peace harnesses the power to change how you think and feel about a circumstance in life—any circumstance.*

This Peace has the power to settle your heart, mind, and soul. This Peace gives you confidence to make courageous, sometimes risky decisions. And conditions don't need to be favorable to experience Peace—that's the best part! In other words, the facts of your dire circumstance don't have to change. Peace will keep your heart light and your mind clear in the stormiest conditions. This kind of Peace also acts as a guide through the challenges of life. We will cover that more in the next chapter.

We won't always be grateful for everything. Ever been thrust awake from a deep sleep due to a cramp in your calf or hamstring muscles? I have! My first response has never been how grateful I was. I don't curse often, but cramps like this encourage it! It's easy to be grateful when someone rubs your feet, you get a raise, your business booms, your child gets straight A's, or you find a $100 bill on the sidewalk. There is power in being grateful in those scenarios, but it doesn't take much intention because it is accompanied with a temporary feeling of happiness.

However, the full power of gratefulness is unleashed when your feet still hurt, you lose your job, your business is failing, your child is struggling in school, or there is more month left than money. It's easy to be grateful when your kids are happy and healthy. It's much harder when one dies unexpectedly. But it is during those really challenging times—times void of a *feeling* of happiness—when an attitude of gratefulness can have the most power to touch and heal our heart, mind, and emotions, and restore our joy.

Some people view their life seeing the glass as half full or half empty. The analogy implies those with a half-full mentality are more optimistic.

That may be true, but there is a superior perspective: A *lifestyle* of gratitude fills the glass to full. That's not to say there isn't more for us to desire, experience, or overcome. But if we lived in a constant state of gratefulness, more is not required to be *content*. Not only will your glass be full—it will pour out with overflow and affect other people.

I would like to think I generally fall into the glass is half full category—maybe even three-quarters full at times. You can ask my wife if you want an accurate evaluation! Regardless, this area of my personal life is primed for growth.

Ask yourself, how often do I feel content with my life? For the overachievers, this is not to say you have stopped dreaming, creating, or looking for the next adventure or conquest. However, it's also not an all-or-nothing proposition. We can live meaningful lives pursuing greatness AND be grateful and content.

There *are* mortal enemies to gratefulness and contentment, the most dangerous of which is the inability to forgive. We can be unwilling to forgive others, situations, and ourselves. It's a trap.

> *Imagine every time you got offended or hurt by someone, you placed a one-pound brick in a backpack you carry every day. One pound is not much. Heck, you might even be able to handle twenty bricks before you notice some drag. Now imagine you never clean this backpack out. It won't be long until the bricks become a real burden. You'll notice that you're now struggling with what once was easy to carry. Your back, neck, and knees may begin to ache, but you don't recognize the correlation with carrying bricks, so you just keep trudging along. If you ignore the pain and continue carrying the bricks, your whole body will suffer because it's now completely out of alignment. What if you only had one brick, but it weighed 100 pounds? I think you get the point. Unforgiveness is like that.*

Here's what the Mayo Clinic Staff had to say about the power of forgiveness from an article written in November 2020:

"Letting go of grudges and bitterness can make way for improved health and peace of mind. Forgiveness can lead to:

- Healthier relationships
- Improved mental health
- Less anxiety, stress, and hostility
- Lower blood pressure
- Fewer symptoms of depression
- A stronger immune system
- Improved heart health
- Improved self-esteem"

I will add that headaches, insomnia, upset stomachs, and asthma are also known to occur more commonly in those living under high levels of stress (particularly those who don't respond well to change or difficult situations). Finding productive ways to release anger, frustration, and other forms of stress—such as letting go of grudges—may mitigate these symptoms.

What many fail to understand is that holding onto anger and being unwilling to forgive only keeps you captive to the person who offended you and the pain they caused. This person we need to forgive is often oblivious to our pain. Or they just … don't care. Forgiveness sets *us* free. It doesn't make what someone did okay, but it does keep us from being a prisoner to the effects of what the person did. That person may even be YOU. A lifestyle of forgiveness positions us to experience true joy, peace, and contentment.

Chapter 5 Reflection

One way to measure contentment is to evaluate different aspects of your life. If there is a glaring deficiency in your marriage, friendships, career, or lifestyle, you likely struggle with something inhibiting your contentment. Learning to be grateful for what you *do* have is a definite key. The ability to stay in a state of peace in every circumstance is another. I will cover more about this in the next chapter. First, here's a quick exercise to evaluate your current contentment in a few key areas of your life.

On a scale of one to ten (ten being highest), give yourself a score in how satisfied you currently are with:

Your life overall.

Your marriage or intimate relationship.

Your friendships.

Your career.

Your financial security.

Having fun.

Your ability to manage your emotions.

Your impact in people's lives.

This simple exercise will help illuminate areas of your life that need attention. Take action now! Enlist your spouse, a dear friend, mentor, or coach to hold you accountable to the improvements you wish to make.

For any category you want to improve, list specific things that would earn a higher score.

Finally, here's a short list of some things we can *all* be grateful for. Feel free to add to this list. I hope these assist you in jumpstarting your ability to express gratefulness every day.

15 Reasons I Am Grateful Every Day

1. I am grateful I woke up this morning and have breath to live another day.

2. I am grateful my basic needs are met.

3. I am grateful I have family and friends.

4. I am grateful I have gainful employment or a business that pays the bills.

5. I am grateful when faced with adversity—it has the potential to grow my character.

6. I am grateful I live in a world with opportunities to chase a dream.

7. I am grateful for the incredible variety of living creatures on Earth. Even wasps and mosquitoes! (This one is tough for me!)

8. I am grateful I live on a beautiful planet with natural wonders all around me.

9. I am grateful for the four seasons of spring, summer, fall, and winter ... each with its own version of weather and beauty. (Unless you live in Texas, where we have two seasons: Hot and freezing. They alternate every few days.)

10. I am grateful advanced technologies make aspects of my life easier and richer.

11. I am grateful advances in transportation have allowed me to explore the world outside my community.

12. I am grateful modern medicine has given me a chance at longer, healthier life.

13. I am grateful I live in a country that values and protects personal freedoms. (I realize this will not be the case for all readers.)

14. I am grateful for the creative abilities of human beings displayed in countless forms.

15. I am grateful for the wonderful diversity of human beings. We are all created with unique features and characteristics that stand out and bring value to the world!

CHAPTER 6

PEACE: A GUIDE THROUGH THE CHAOS

Back in 2005, Amárillys and I faced a series of difficult decisions. I had resigned from a position at a large international ministry, and we were convinced something exciting was on the other side of that choice. Amárillys and I were taking a leap of faith. And so, I started to follow specific instructions we felt God was giving us.

His first instructions were terms I needed to give my employer. I submitted a thirty-day notice so I could have ample time to train my replacements and leave them on good footing before I left. I did not have another position to transition to, so there was no urgency. In fact, part of our instruction was that once I was unemployed, I would not apply to any new positions for another thirty days. I had traveled extensively and been away from home a lot in the last few years. God told me to spend the month with my wife and two boys, focused on being a family.

Of course, with the understanding that I would have no income that month, virtually no one else saw this as a sound strategy. When I quit, my employer was clearly not obligated to pay me a severance, nor did we expect one. But *we* had inner peace. We obeyed, despite the risk that was compounded with the fact Amárillys was a stay-at-home mom and we had a house mortgage and car payments to make.

Once we acted on the decision, a series of miracles unfolded—*slowly*. When I submitted the notice to my boss, he expressed great concern. After years of working together, Jon was more than just who I reported to—he was also a dear, trusted friend who cared deeply for my family. He wished I had a tangible plan and was uneasy about me leaving without a severance package. He mentioned something about seeing what he could do. I didn't anticipate anything, though I appreciated his kind gesture.

Fast forward to two days before the end of my thirty-day notice. Jon called me into the office. He expressed appreciation for my hard work and said he had gone to battle for me. Even though receiving a severance package after quitting was unheard of, he had managed to get me one month's severance. I was blown away! God's instruction to stay home for the next month and not look for work had become a much more palatable prospect.

The next day, I went through the typical last-day motions with my colleagues. We ate cake and exchanged many kind words and hugs. Jon texted me near the end of the day. He was on his way to Belgium and could not participate in my send-off. He had one last thing to say before I was no longer an employee. The text read something like: "Check that, I got you six weeks' severance." Wow! I was amazed and grateful. The severance would be paid out over three biweekly payroll cycles.

I spent the next month as ordered, not seeking employment. I spent time with Amárillys, Gabriel, and Joel. We did DIY home projects and enjoyed life without all the travel and fast pace. As you might surmise, the thirty days went by quickly. Time flies when you're having fun and don't have a job! I was now clear to search for the next big thing, so I began submitting my resume. I was not driven to be a pastor or even in ministry. Most of the jobs I applied for were corporate types, with a few exceptions.

One day, while trolling websites of large ministries I was familiar with, I felt compelled to pull up Jesse Duplantis Ministries in Louisiana. I was *not* looking for a job. Hurricane Katrina had devastated Southeast Louisiana just six months prior, so I was curious how they were doing. I watched a video update and then flippantly clicked the Job Opportunities tab. I still don't know why. There was a listing for a youth pastor. Amárillys was sitting behind me, so I quickly turned and said with a hint of sarcasm, "Jesse Duplantis is looking for a youth pastor." As I turned back, she said something I never would have expected: "Why don't you apply?"

Ha, funny! Let me list a few reasons why that was ridiculous. First, I was forty years old and had never attended a youth service in my life! In my opinion, I was grossly unqualified. Add to that the fact I wasn't even sure if I wanted to be *any* kind of pastor. As I mentioned, Hurricane Katrina had turned the region upside down. It was still a mess. We loved living in McKinney, Texas and had bought our first home there two years prior. That seemed like enough reason to not apply for the position. And perhaps most importantly, we had family and lots of friends in the Dallas Metroplex. We didn't know anyone in the entire state of Louisiana! We also loved our church, Covenant Church in Carrollton, Texas. *Surely,* she was joking. I asked, "Do *you* want to move to Louisiana?" "No," she replied. "But shouldn't we let God guide us?"

I wasn't fazed, but I also couldn't argue with that. I quickly gave in, attaching my resume to an email. Then I said a prayer about as fervently as I would blessing a bowl of Fruit Loops for breakfast, and I hit send. There! It was in His hands now—I could move on. I sincerely felt there was ZERO chance I'd get a call.

You've probably already guessed where this is going. A couple weeks went by, and I received a call. "This is Pastor David Salstrand from Covenant Church," the caller said. He kept talking, but I was distracted. My mind raced. I wondered, *Who is this guy? How did I not know he was on staff at our church?* (I didn't know yet that the name of the Duplantis' church was the same as our home church.) Then he said the word *resume,* and my attention thrust back into the conversation. I suddenly realized what was happening. He was the acting Senior Pastor and wanted to conduct an interview!

We had a brief conversation about my background and what I knew about their church. Since that basically amounted to *nada*, I expected nothing more than a polite end to the call. Plus, I had a big softball game to get to!

Instead, Pastor David extended an invitation to pay for our flight so we could come down for an interview. I was honored that someone would go to the expense of buying plane tickets just to talk to us, so I accepted. My soul was still in a place of perfect peace. In my mind, we would just enjoy going on a little trip so we could check this off the list of possibilities.

Upon arriving in New Orleans, we were picked up and driven to the church by Pastor David and his wife, Betty. Our first interaction with the church staff could not have been more awkward. It had nothing to do with them—they were all very kind and hospitable. The issue was our attire. We'd dressed like the pastoral staff at our home church on a Sunday. I was decked out in a shiny grey suit and silk tie, which had been custom made for me while traveling in Seoul, Korea. Meanwhile, Amárillys was wearing her Sunday best as well, minus a big hat. Everyone there was dressed very casually, making us stand out like a sore thumb. *See,* I thought. *This is proof we're a terrible fit for this place.*

The interview process continued throughout the day, and I couldn't help but notice David and Betty were using a lot of statements that in sales are called *assumptive closes*. They were talking like we were already hired! Phrases like "This is your office," and "When you move here." It was becoming clear they really believed this fit could work!

The battle to keep my peace was beginning. On the return flight to Dallas, we talked about what we'd just experienced. The church had lost about half of its congregation due to people fleeing the region before Katrina, many of whom never returned. Countless people who remained had lost their homes, possessions, jobs, and even loved ones. Many were emotionally and spiritually broken. We both agreed there was great need. Then a strange thing happened. We began to weep. We felt God tugging our heartstrings.

There was still a significant hurdle remaining. We had not met with Jesse and Cathy Duplantis, the founders of the church. They were the final decision makers and had to sign off on me being hired. I remained confident that this was little more than an obedience exercise. They would not offer me the position.

Well, a week or so went by, and Pastor David called back. They DID want to hire us! After some discussion and working through all the practical reasons why we should say no, we decided to say yes. I called back and gave Pastor David my word, and we put together a loose plan of when we would start. Despite the move, and despite the job being something I'd never imagined or strived for, I once again felt at peace.

The peace wouldn't last long.

I had not shared the news with my mentor and pastor, Gordon Banks. He had been out of the country during our trip, and he didn't return until after I had verbally accepted the position. *No problem*, I thought. *He'll be so excited for us!* I was wrong. I called him to give him the great news, and his first response was, "You didn't sign anything, did you?" He was clearly unnerved and disappointed I had not talked to him before accepting the position. I was confused by his reaction, especially since it sounded like he wanted me to call them back and tell them I had changed my mind. I objected, telling him, "I gave them my word." After agreeing to eventually meet in person, our call ended. I was distraught and completely caught off guard. Amárillys had to coax me off the proverbial ledge. I reconciled that there was no way I would go back on my word, but that if we had made the wrong decision, then God would have them retract their offer.

I saw Pastor Gordon in person a few days later. Despite agreeing to meet in person eventually, we had not scheduled this meeting. I had come to attend a youth service so I could see what one looked like now that it appeared I was going to be a youth pastor!

We spoke in the hallway in front of the youth room. He seemed even more convinced that we were not going anywhere, even comparing our situation to that of Abraham and Isaac's from the Bible. If you are not familiar with the story, here it is in short: Abraham and his wife Sarah did not have a child (Isaac) until they were in their nineties. Then, when Isaac had become a young man, God commanded Abraham to take him to a holy mountain and sacrifice him! They would pack up their belongings and servants and travel for a few days to the appointed destination. But in the eleventh hour, just before Abraham fulfilled the request, God stopped the process and provided a ram as a substitute sacrifice for Isaac. Abraham had passed the test of obedience and God released him to a far more palatable destiny. According to Pastor Gordon, I was now Abraham. God would release me from my commitment and provide another opportunity. The conversation ended at that—abruptly! I was stunned once again. Peace was eluding me.

The next day, a friend on staff at our church gave me some insider information. Apparently in the few weeks prior to our trip to Louisiana, Pastor Gordon and our senior pastor, Mike Hayes, had discussed where I might fit into the organization in the future. Behind closed doors they were looking into the possibility of creating a position to bring me on board. Suddenly his reaction made much more sense! It was a huge honor. And if it had come sooner, I would have jumped at the opportunity. But the strange thing was, once I understood what was going on and prayed about it, my soul returned to a state of peace. More importantly, Amárillys and I *both* had peace in the fact that we were indeed moving to Louisiana.

Since I am using this story to illustrate how supernatural Peace guides you, allow me to recap a couple of things and add some new information. The environmental conditions in the greater New Orleans area were not good. The massive flooding had caused many long-term effects including debris from homes, crippled businesses, deceased wildlife, mold, and more. The housing market was razor-thin, with many homes and apartments having been destroyed. This had caused housing prices to skyrocket due to a lack of inventory. Many stores and restaurants that physically remained were still closed or had limited hours.

As I said before, we didn't know anyone in Southeast Louisiana. Where we lived in McKinney, the city pulsed with exciting growth. We had a great church, friends, and family nearby. Did I mention that I didn't even know how much my salary would be? Crazy, I know. But that was also part of the instructions we felt we received from God. He told me not to ask, for He would take care of us. I had never approached a new job like that before. And I don't recommend you do either—unless you're certain God has instructed you to. Despite many signs that pointed to staying in McKinney, we were at total peace with our decision to leave. Here is how this principle reads in the biblical text:

> *"Do not be anxious about anything, but in everything by prayer and supplication with thanksgiving let your requests be made known to God. And **the peace of God**, which surpasses all understanding, will guard your hearts and your minds in Christ Jesus."*
> *Philippians 4:6-7 ESV*

Let me describe what this looks like when applied. We are not cursed to reside in a state of anxiety or chaos. We have the privilege of being able to converse with God about our life, and I am grateful for the relationship. When I ask for direction, I find Peace (not worry or confusion) in the answer He has given me. This Peace will allow me to have His thoughts and perspective on what I should do, and my heart will be settled. I'll know the decision is best for me and my family. In other words, Peace directs me when I am confronted with a decision or path that at first glimpse looks like something I would not normally choose. Peace provides courage to take risks—*divinely calculated* risks. Peace also works this way when conditions are favorable, and when your desires and thoughts align.

Let's take a quick rabbit trail. A couple of years after we began our journey in Louisiana, an opportunity arose to be reunited with Pastors Gordon and Derozette Banks, whom I mentioned earlier. They had left Dallas and become senior pastors of a church in a small city in between Tacoma and Seattle, Washington. We took a short vacation to visit them during Christmas break. Upon our return, they asked us to consider coming on staff and helping them with their new endeavor. The opportunity was exciting, and we felt an immediate connection with the people we'd met while there.

The Banks had been our primary mentors for years. They had a major influence on us individually and in our marriage. We had conversations with God about the move because it seemed *too easy*. It has been my experience that the plans I have drawn up at times are not the ones God has for me. Things usually work out different than I expected, and His plan always turns out better than my own.

I have found it's sometimes harder to discern where the Peace is in a situation when it's something I *want* to do versus something I *would not* have chosen first. In this case, Peace guided us to Seattle. We knew it was the right move. We would spend the next seven years there. That season of our lives was beautiful, and it caused us to grow in many ways we would not have elsewhere. My point? When you find the true compass Peace reveals, you can't lose!

Back to Louisiana. Remember, we were moving to a chaotic environment without a place to live, with no friends, and we didn't know what my salary would be! We predicted it would be a pay cut from the position I had resigned from; we just didn't know *how much less* I would earn. Still, we jumped headfirst into our new role.

Our first act would be to drive several hours from our home in McKinney to a camp outside of Houston that our new youth group had already made plans to attend. It was strange meeting most of our youth for the first time at a neutral site. But all in all, it was a great week.

After the camp, we drove back home (our housing situation was not settled yet, and we hadn't decided whether to rent or sell our house in McKinney). Our second week on the job, I would fly to Louisiana alone to work in the office and lead my first youth service. Upon arriving at the airport, I was picked up by Pastor David. On the drive to the church, he told me, "Oh, by the way, we already put you on the payroll. I have a check waiting for you when we get there." Fantastic, I was relieved to know we were getting paid! But there was much more significance pertaining to the *timing* of this first check.

You'll recall my writing that the severance I received was paid out biweekly over a six-week period. Are you ready for how amazing things can go when you learn to follow God's Peace? It turned out that the pay cycles from my previous employer and my new one were the same. I should also mention that my new employer knew nothing about my severance, let alone when it would end! So, the check I would receive came on the EXACT SAME day I'd receive my final severance payment! We had stepped out in faith, followed the Peace of God, trusted our needs would be met, and because of it we didn't miss a single day of income! Amazing, right?

How much of a pay cut did I take? Initially, a little under $10,000 a year. Bummer, huh? Not really. Six short months later, I was called into the senior pastor's office. After sitting down, I was told that Jesse and Cathy Duplantis had recognized Amárillys and I were already taking on more responsibility than we were hired for, and that we were bringing a lot of value to their staff. They felt a raise was not appropriate given I had been on staff less than the typical one-year required for a rating review, which one needed for consideration for a pay *raise*.

Instead, they gave me an immediate salary adjustment of 33%! That's right—I'd gone from a pay cut to making more than I had with my previous employer! Does that knowledge encourage you?

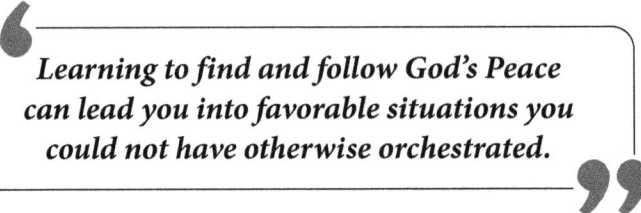

Learning to find and follow God's Peace can lead you into favorable situations you could not have otherwise orchestrated.

Our housing was taken care of (we had a beautiful home and lot on the bayou, which is still our favorite of all the homes we lived in), my income increased, and we were stretched and growing in our new role. And eventually, we made many lifelong friends and developed real impact in the lives that we touched.

There are some simple things you can do to increase your odds of staying in a state of peace on a consistent basis. Here they are.

Chapter 6 Reflection

Keys to Living at Peace

- Get ample sleep. Well-rested humans find it much easier to remain in a state of peace.

- Set aside time daily to sit quietly, meditate, or pray. Doing so first thing in the morning is most effective since it will set the tone for your day. If early doesn't work, find time elsewhere, but make it a priority!

- Set aside time weekly to decompress and think. Going for a walk is one great way to do this!

- Be quick to forgive (we covered this in an earlier chapter). Traveling light in your heart is critical in maintaining your peace.

- When making a tough decision, create a list of pros and cons to sort the facts and uncover things warranting consideration.

- Collect stories of God carrying you through hard times. Borrow other people's stories when you lack your own to draw back on.

- Express gratitude often (discussed in the previous chapter).

- Minimize or eliminate watching the news.

- Get as healthy as possible. Work out. Eat well. This will strengthen your body and brain while minimizing health concerns that can steal your peace.

- Get wise counsel from trusted sources who have *successfully* navigated rough waters. At all costs, avoid involving people in a decision if they do not have a great track record. Example: getting marriage advice from someone in an unhealthy marriage or from someone who's been through a bitter divorce (or three)!

- Limit how many people you receive counsel from. Too many can bring confusion and rattle your peace.

- Be judicious when seeking counsel from people with a vested interest in your decision.

Now, make a list to examine things (or people!) that steal your peace. Are there some you can eliminate today?

Peace is a powerful force. It has helped Amárillys and I navigate difficult decisions, troubled waters, and unity in our marriage. It's guided us in managing our emotions and healing from the tragic loss of our oldest son. It can be your Guide too!

CHAPTER 7
A LESSON IN COLLABORATION

IN THE SUMMER of 2012, I accepted speaking engagements at two churches in Eastern Washington. The first was in Spokane. We had a wonderful time at the church service, hanging out with the pastors and staff and enjoying the beautiful surroundings. On our way back from Spokane, we stopped at the other church in Moses Lake. Again, we had a powerful experience at the church and thoroughly enjoyed meeting some amazing people after the evening service.

We didn't need to be back at our home church until the next evening, which afforded us plenty of time before we had to leave the next day. We were invited by the pastor and his wife to go wakeboarding the next morning on Moses Lake. One of their church members lived on the lake and had offered to take us out on their boat and teach us the sport.

The morning weather was perfect! It was warm but not too hot. And it was a Monday, so the water was smooth like glass because there was little activity. I wasn't interested in wakeboarding (I had attempted it years before and failed epically) but Amárillys eagerly jumped into the water. She had never tried before, so she was very excited. Oh, and she's very competitive! This was going to be fun!

A Lesson in Collaboration

On her first attempt, Amárillys popped right up out of the water but accidentally let go of the rope. She immediately sank before she could get going. I raised the red flag to signal to other boaters that someone was in the water as we circled back. "One more time!" she shouted. We all yelled in return "You got this!"

As she bobbed in the water, the driver straightened the boat and Amárillys got into position. As instructed, she gave a thumbs up when she was ready, and I yelled, "Hit it!" This attempt lasted less than three seconds. I had been shooting a video on my phone, and all I saw was her pop up for just a second, fight to get straight, and then with a jarring thud flip forward into the water. She was so close! I raised the red flag again to signify she was down. As the driver turned the boat to circle back, I could faintly hear Amárillys screaming under the sound of the motor. At first it sounded like a scream of frustration—appropriate given her competitiveness. But as we got closer and the driver pulled back on the motor, I could hear she was still screaming. Her cries were the sound of desperation. About thirty feet out from her, I could finally make out her words. "I think I broke my leg!" she was yelling in a bloodcurdling tone!

I immediately was in the water, swimming towards her as fast as I could. I was not prepared for what I would find. Once I was next to her, I looked at her legs and couldn't believe my eyes. Her right leg was grossly twisted and distorted in the thigh area, swollen beyond comprehension. She was in a lot of pain, and her feet were still in the boots of the wakeboard. It was terrifying to behold.

She was in serious trouble, and we had to act fast. Though she was trying to cooperate and remain calm, she couldn't help but push me down into the water a couple of times as I tried to hold her still. Swimming back to the boat was a delicate process. I had to make sure her leg didn't move more than necessary and cause more pain than she was already in. Lifting her into the boat without doing that would be impossible. We did the best we could to minimize her duress. As gently as we could, we lifted her into the back of the boat.

Everyone on the boat saw the horror of what had happened. There was no time to talk. Thank God, the owner of the boat happened to be a registered nurse. We all knew we had to get Amárillys medical care ASAP. We were about a thirty-minute drive from the hospital, so calling an ambulance was not a reasonable option. It was obvious from the massive swelling in her thigh that she was possibly experiencing internal bleeding. Our boat driver switched fully into ER nurse mode and began to tell us what needed to happen next. I will never forget the calm demeanor everyone displayed. I have no doubt the others were fighting to not reveal their panic, just as I was. We tried hard not to let Amárillys sense that.

The first task was to get her stabilized for transport. Good fortune was on our side—we were at the boat owner's personal dock, where crucial supplies were already on site. We pulled the back seat from the boat to use as a makeshift stretcher. It was the perfect length and width! We then began the very delicate task of anchoring Amárillys to it. The process went quickly, smoother than you could have imagined. A life vest was wrapped around her leg to cushion her and keep the leg slightly elevated. We then gathered tie-down straps that were used to secure her body to the "stretcher." I ran to our Honda Odyssey minivan and feverishly removed the third-row seat. I then folded down the second row to make room for Amárillys. We cautiously slid her into the van and were immediately relieved—she fit perfectly. Our friend Theresa jumped in the back, I rushed to the driver's seat, and we were off!

With my heart racing, I stepped on the gas. There was a fine line between getting to the hospital quickly and not jerking the car around and causing Amárillys any more discomfort than she was already in. The thirty-minute drive only took about twenty, and upon arriving at the emergency room entrance we frantically employed the assistance of the doctors and nurses on duty. The staff worked to get her into a room and start diagnosing the situation. It was vividly evident that she had suffered a severe fracture of her right femur. What was impossible to detect was if there was any *life-threatening* internal bleeding. The nurses did their best to keep Amárillys as comfortable as possible while they placed her into a traction device. At the same time, a plan for what to do next was being formed. I implored them to give her some pain medication but was ensured that it was better right now to make sure she stayed awake and alert. My heart sunk again for my beautiful bride. This was a freaking nightmare!

It was decided that her injury would require major surgery, which was beyond the scope of the small-town hospital. Plans were set in motion to acquire an ambulance and rush us to the city of Bellevue, where she would receive the care she desperately needed. This might sound like a relief, but we were in Eastern Washington. Bellevue was 172 miles away—a three-hour drive back to Western Washington! I'll admit, fear was trying to crush my faith that everything would be okay. Transporting her was our only option. Within about an hour, she was loaded into the ambulance, and we took off.

I trailed the ambulance in our Odyssey and did the only thing I could—pray! About an hour or two into the drive, we were making good time. But suddenly, we were dealt yet another devastating blow. The primary interstate from Western to Eastern Washington is I-90. It is well traveled by commuters, vacationers, and tractor trailers delivering goods across the state. It was August, the peak of summertime, so we did not have to navigate potential snow delays. Traveling this time of year is typically fast and smooth. However, aside from a car accident, there is one other event that can slow you down.

We came to a sudden stop. Looking ahead, cars were backed up as far as we could see. I stepped out of the car and talked with the paramedics. They had already confirmed the shutdown. The Washington State Department of Transportation was doing rock blasting up ahead. If you are not familiar with rock blasting, this is a technique used to break up the rocky mountainside with controlled explosives to widen and expand the existing highway. We were aware of the practice, but today of all days was the worst timing ever. Estimated delay: one hour! "You have got to be kidding me," I said, maybe even uttering a couple of curse words. We were a little more than an hour out from our destination, and completely stuck.

The paramedics opened the back of the ambulance and left the doors open so Amárillys and I could talk freely. By now she had been given a low dose of pain medication, but it was not enough. She was in a lot of pain, especially her right foot due to the constant pull of the traction device used to keep her femur bone from moving or shifting. It was heartbreaking. I don't remember what we talked about. I only remember trying to comfort and encourage her. Time had crawled to a screeching halt, and the hour felt much longer than normal. Our faith was still intact, but it was being tested, hard! I couldn't help but silently ask, "God, can't you do something to speed this up?" He didn't, and after the predicted hour we were finally on our way to Bellevue again.

We arrived safely and were whisked into a temporary room to await a meeting with the surgeon. Amárillys was still in a lot of pain, but being in a safe place at least brought a measure of calm. By now our senior pastors, Gordon and Derozette Banks, had arrived as well. Having some friendly faces was comforting, and our faith that everything would be fine began to rise again. Adding to our encouragement was that the surgeon was considered one of the best—if not *the* best—in the country for this type of surgery. He had recently moved from Atlanta, the city in the United States with the highest rate of severe femur fractures at the time. Curious, I asked why? The answer was simple. Atlanta, which like a lot of large cities has major traffic issues, had the most side impact car accidents in the country. That's the most common cause of a complete femur break (due to the blunt force trauma). He had a lot of practice before coming to Washington! Maybe God was moving after all?

The surgery went perfectly, and the surgeon returned to the waiting room to give me an update. Amárillys had suffered what is called a spiral fracture. A spiral fracture occurs when a long bone is torn in half by a twisting force or impact. It's gruesome and can have dangerous complications. The way her femur broke was very fortunate—a piece of the bone hadn't nicked a major artery. If it had, she could've bled out. This was especially lucky given how long it took us to get her to the appropriate hospital. For us, it was not just good fortune. It was a miracle. It confirmed that God had his hand on the situation.

Rehab was going to be long and arduous. We were told it would be at least five months before she could bear any weight on her leg. That meant she couldn't put her foot down, and she certainly couldn't drive. We had a two-story home, and our bedroom was upstairs—not ideal. Couple that with the fact our boys were young and energetic. Gabriel was eleven, Joel eight, and Liam a rambunctious three. Liam would present the biggest challenge as he loved to cuddle up with mommy. Managing her living conditions and creating a comfortable and safe environment for recovery was our highest priority. But it wasn't the only one.

Amárillys required hands-on care and help with feeding her, assisting her to the bathroom, getting into bed, and everything in between. How in the world could I do that and fulfill my role as the youth and young adults pastor?

I couldn't. In fact, I would need help from the boys and many others to navigate the season we were thrust into. It felt impossible, like nothing good could come out of all the chaos. I was wrong.

When it came to building teams, I was a champion of giving people the opportunity to have a meaningful role and use their gifts and talents. Regarding things I thought were my sole responsibility, I was a control freak. I loved to rally around others when they were in a tough spot. I always encouraged my team to avoid taking on more than they could handle and to let others help when they were overwhelmed with life. But I was terrible at following my own advice. When I needed to delegate a task I considered my responsibility, I typically clenched it with a death grip. In caring for Amárillys, I learned the beautiful concept of collaboration in a meaningful way—and out of necessity, not choice.

If you want to live a **Big, Bold, Brave** life, I have news for you: You can't do it alone. Whether you want to have a massive influence on the world around you or get through difficult circumstances, you will need help. Collaboration is powerful, and it is as old as the hills.

In the biblical scriptures, we see countless examples of greatness being achieved through collaboration. And while individuals are often the ones honored (and perhaps revered more by history), none accomplished their amazing feats alone. Here is a short list:

We would not revere ...

Moses without collaboration from Aaron, Miriam, Caleb, and Joshua.

David without Jonathan and his Mighty Men.

Esther without Mordecai or vice versa.

Gideon without his 300 Men of Valor.

Paul without Barnabas and Timothy.

Even Jesus recruited twelve disciples, sent out the seventy-two, and collaborates with you and I today.

But you don't have to be religious to see the benefits of collaboration. Just look at the multitude of musical artists who collaborate on projects. I especially love it when they seem like unlikely collaborators. To name just one track, Justin Timberlake and Chris Stapleton's *Say Something* yielded incredible results. Here's another short list of great collaborators:

Steve Jobs and Steve Wozniak (along with countless employees) created the Apple empire.

Orville and Wilbur Wright—together the first to prove flying a fixed-wing aircraft was possible.

Paul McCartney, John Lennon, Ringo Starr, George Harrison, and producer George Martin changed modern music forever.

Larry Page and Sergey Brin founded a company that touches every corner of the world—Google.

Helen Keller and Anne Sullivan's work together radically changed the educational opportunities for the deaf and blind.

There were countless others involved behind the scenes in each of these successes. If you're going to do something great and impact the world, you must embrace collaboration. We were not created to succeed in life without comingling with others.

During the five months Amárillys was rehabbing, many adjustments had to be made in how we approached life and ministry. These changes started at home. The boys had to chip in with simple chores around the house, which typically either Amárillys or I would've taken care of. This included picking up toys, keeping their rooms clean (not surgery room sterile, just not a pigsty), making simple breakfasts, and perhaps the most critical task, not running over mommy! The boys handled it all surprisingly well. They were real troopers! We would have never chosen what led to this emerging teamwork, but the changes it forced us to make jelled us as a family unit. We were in it together. I believe this was the beginning of a foundation we built as a family that would serve us well in the years ahead as we faced adversity together head on, including the tragedy of losing Gabriel.

Our church and volunteer staff were incredibly supportive and sensitive to our situation. Our youth ministry team—comprised mostly of volunteers ranging from their late teens to twenties—was especially amazing. Some led departments such as worship, outreach, hospitality, sound, and media, and most led a small group of teenagers.

We had to lean on them more than ever, and they were pressed into leading their areas more autonomously. They met the challenge and exceeded our expectations. The departments executed their functions better than ever. It's probably more accurate to say they *carried us*!

We had developed a speaking team of eight gifted young leaders who were honing their skills. I typically spoke three out of four Wednesday nights (our largest single attendance was on these nights) and during most of our two Sunday services. With Amárillys' injury, I had to cut back dramatically for a while. Our young leaders picked up the slack. Given extra space and responsibility, they grew exponentially in their gifts. It was amazing watching them thrive. In our absence, they stepped up to the plate and hit the proverbial ball out of the park.

We were so grateful and proud of them. I learned a lot about servant leadership, collaboration, and frankly, how blind I was to some of my control freak tendencies. Amárillys eventually got back on her feet, and our personal lives returned to normal. But the changes we were forced to make transformed our youth ministry and team. We would never be the same, and that was a good thing! Permanent changes were implemented, and I scaled back speaking on Sundays to once a quarter. We were still the leaders of the ministry, but our success was attributed to the passion, skill, and faithfulness of our team.

One more unexpected byproduct arose (this will help those of you who lead organizations or groups). In allowing our team to collaborate in significant ways *with us*, the team leaders began to collaborate much more effectively with *each other*. This way of leading produces servant leaders, rather than employees or mercenaries ready to change sides for a better offer.

Servant Leadership – Prolific Collaborators

Let's discuss attributes of a servant leader. After all, servant leaders are prolific collaborators. Here are some qualities they exude:

A servant leader actively seeks to help with areas of need that arise in their circle of influence. They sometimes delay their own desires or goals for the good of the whole.

Servant leaders look for win-win outcomes whenever possible. Personal success does not overshadow an opportunity to help others win.

A servant leader gets their hands dirty and leads others by example, not by compulsion.

A servant leader does the right thing for the right reason. They are not intoxicated by approval or praise.

A servant leader is intentional in showing appreciation and value for others. They desire the same in return, but don't demand it.

A servant leader is a natural gatherer and encourager of people.

A servant leader is an active listener. They seek to understand. They are not driven to be heard or proven right.

Servant leaders are passionate. They trust it is inevitable the right people will join their side and vision. They are not bitter towards those with a different purpose.

A servant leader is a tenacious problem solver. They value other people's insights and experiences; solutions can come from any source. Their satisfaction comes from solving the problem, not getting the credit for it.

Servant leaders are secure people confident in the value they bring. They are comfortable not being the smartest person in the room. In fact, they embrace great thinkers and creatives.

Servant leaders don't expose the inadequacies or faults of others to look superior. They are quick to uplift, encourage, coach, and even cover others' mistakes when appropriate.

A servant leader has a father or mother's heart. In their circle of influence, they are focused on building a family, not an infrastructure built on the backs of people. They prioritize their business, organization, or relationships in this order: people first, process second, and product/results last.

THIS NEXT ONE IS HUGE!

> *A servant leader searches for the gold in people. They are not jaded by the shortcomings of other humans. They see the potential in everyone, and they help excavate it.*

Great marriages reflect a beautifully orchestrated collaboration between husband and wife. A tightknit, loving family exists because of the collaborative nature of those within the family unit. We celebrate sports teams that win a championship at their respective pinnacle of achievement. Their success is a result of effective collaboration. What about individual sports such as wrestling, tennis, skiing, or snowboarding? While these athletes thrive relying on their individual performance for success, collaboration is still necessary for them to reach their peak. At minimum they have coaches, mentors, training partners, or teammates playing an integral part in their training to reach peak performance.

> *There is nothing more rewarding than accomplishing great feats with the help of others. The reward is amplified because a multitude gets to share in the accolades.*

There are many great books that illustrate how servant leadership uses collaboration to achieve extraordinary results. One of my favorites was written by the man who penned the foreword for this book, Howard Behar. *It's Not About the Coffee* describes how the model of servant leadership and putting people first was a major catalyst for the explosive growth that led Starbucks to becoming a global brand by building community. I highly recommend you pick it up!

Creativity thrives in a collaborative setting. Every human is as unique as the colors in a kaleidoscope. We were divinely created that way and meant to stand out AND complement one another. I implore you, don't live an isolated life restrained by your own limitations. Be a champion of others. **Big, Bold, Brave** humans seek to make connections. They take risks and invite others into their personal journey.

Chapter 7 Reflection

Think about the people in your life ...

Describe the meaningful ways you collaborate within these relationships.

What relationships do you currently have where collaboration would add greater value to each of your lives?

How many of the servant-leadership attributes mentioned in this chapter do you actively employ in ...

Your marriage?

Your family?

Your friendships?

Your job?

Your business?

How could you intentionally apply a servant-leader mentality in other settings, including ...

Your kids' school, sports teams, or clubs?

While shopping at a grocery store or mall?

In your church?

Volunteering in your community?

Within an organization you are a part of or support?

Chapter 8

Fear, Less!

GABRIEL DIED ON September 23, 2019. A few months later, everyone on the planet had their world rocked. In early January 2020, I came down with a weird illness I had never experienced before. I had congestion in my sinuses and chest, significant fatigue, and an annoying cough. But the symptom that really threw me off was that I lost all sense of taste and smell. That had never happened before. (Well, except for the time I snorted a beaker of ammonia against the advice of my high school chemistry teacher. A story for another day. Let's just say I'm lucky I can still smell!)

As January rolled on, news began to stretch across the globe about a new virus that was spreading. When the list of symptoms was released, I realized I must have had this new virus. By then, our entire household had been through it and had quickly recovered. Our government instituted the "Thirty Days to Slow the Spread" initiative, which included terms we are all now very familiar with: social distancing, masks, testing, quarantines, and vaccines. Regardless of your personal position on how or if these measures should have been implemented, I have yet to talk to anyone that doesn't agree fear spread on a global scale unlike anything we have seen before. It quite literally changed the world.

The following statement is not meant to be political. I will share my personal position on combating the onslaught of *fear* brought on by the pandemic. It's the same way we process and combat ANY fear, and how we all face fears! At times, being fearful is a good thing. Here's a little science to clarify.

Fear comes from the brain.

When people encounter something that frightens them, the hypothalamus in the brain reacts by releasing a series of chemicals to the sympathetic nervous system and the adrenal-cortical system. In the sympathetic nervous system, signals are sent out to release "stress hormones" like adrenaline. These kick the body into high gear, so it becomes tense and alert. At the same time, the adrenal-cortical system is also secreting hormones to other parts of the body, which instigates a series of remarkable, almost instantaneous, changes. Heart rate and blood pressure increase, pupils dilate to take in as much light as possible, nonessential systems such as the immune system and digestion turn themselves off to allow more energy to go towards emergency function, and veins in the skin constrict to keep blood in the major muscle groups. It becomes difficult to focus on small tasks since your brain is preoccupied with the fear. *(Science World* article: Friday, October 27, 2017)

Altogether, this is known as the fight-flight-freeze response. While the fight-flight-freeze response causes various physiological reactions, it's *triggered* by a psychological fear.

The fear is conditioned, meaning you've associated a situation or thing with negative experiences. This psychological response develops over time and is initiated when you're first exposed to the situation. The thing you're scared of is called a *perceived threat* (something you consider to be dangerous). Perceived threats are different for each person.

When you're faced with a perceived threat, your brain thinks you're in danger. That's because it already considers the situation to be life threatening. As a result, your body automatically reacts with the fight-flight-freeze response to keep you safe. If I encounter a bear in the woods (which I have), I will experience a legitimate fear of getting mauled and eaten! When facing possible harm or death, we switch into survival mode. Science shows that our brain processes information very quickly.

My personal encounter with bears occurred on a camping trip on Shasta Lake in Redding, California. Around 3 a.m., I stepped out of my tent with a flashlight in hand to go to the bathroom. I walked towards the area where we had built a high-class latrine—okay, we dug a hole—to get a few feet away from the tent. I'd only moved a few steps before I realized my friend Chris had also come out of his tent, which was about twenty feet away.

Chris saw my flashlight and turned his attention to me. "There's a bear over there," he yell-whispered. My immediate reaction was disbelief. Not that the situation could occur, but that he was telling the truth. Chris was a bit of a truth-stretcher. Fact-checking him was always a good idea. I cupped my mouth with my hands and yell-whispered back, "No way!" Then he pointed his flashlight in the direction of the latrine. Sure enough, there were *two* black bears! One was a full-grown mama, probably weighing in around 200 pounds, while the baby was much smaller. However, in the dark, mama looked the size of a Kodiak, which range between 400-700 pounds! Black bears are generally not a threat to attack. But a mama protecting her baby is a little more unpredictable.

The thought occurred to me that Chris was much closer to them. If I kept my distance and she decided to attack, Chris could keep her *busy* while I made my escape! (Just kidding. Sort of.) Chris was also a little, well, psycho. I couldn't rule out him attacking the mama! The bears quickly slipped off into the darkness, but we could hear their paws stepping on twigs and branches. It sounded like they might be attempting to circle around us, so we sprang into action. Our brains led us to stoke and reignite the still-flickering campfire, which we would stay near until dawn. We thought it would deter the bears, knowledge we'd both heard somewhere. I have since found out it's not true—the bears only left of their own accord. So, don't accept our fire-starting technique as sound survival advice. You're better off making noise like singing a campfire song loud and off-key. I could have executed that technique with precision! Despite my poor survival skills, you are reading this book because I thankfully lived another day. My memory has faded a little—did I see Chris again once daylight came? Hmm?

The kind of fear we experienced is *natural* fear. It's in our DNA. We experienced fear that provoked us to act and get out of an immediate and potentially dangerous situation. But there is other forms of fear I consider *unnatural*. They attack your spirit, emotions, and thoughts with the goal of crippling you. That's the fear Amárillys and I vehemently despise! Let's talk about that kind of fear.

Our experiences tend to shape how we see the world. Interestingly enough, a life experience can be considered negative or destructive, and yet humans don't all respond to them in the same way. These experiences can stop us in our tracks due to fear of an imaginary bad outcome or stir us up to battle and overcome every obstacle. Humans who face their fears will win huge victories—for themselves AND for others!

Meet my new friend, Blake. He graduated magna cum laude with a degree in marketing and a minor in Spanish after just three and a half years. Since then, he has been able to work in industries he's passionate about. As an athlete, he gets to represent his country and play at the highest level. Blake has a passion for videography and photography. Oh, and he just got married in July 2021! You might be wondering, how is his story relevant to fear? Glad you asked!

You see, about six years ago, at the age of sixteen, Blake lost most of his central vision due to a genetic condition called LHON. The condition caused him to become legally blind and have a visual acuity of around 20/800. Yes, 20/800, that is not a typo! I love how Blake describes his condition, which could have been a devastating defeat to most humans. He says, "In spite of—no, *because* of—the challenges that I've faced through my vision loss, I have been able to accomplish all those amazing things."

When Blake's vision loss first developed, he was overwhelmed with doubts about his life. He wasn't sure how he'd be able to continue doing what he loved. But through passion, gaining a new perspective, and the encouragement from those around him, he learned he could continue to do the same things. Frankly, he could do *way more*, just in a different way. School came with many challenges—having to learn new technology like magnification and screen reading software—but it gave Blake the grit and determination to continue pursuing what he loved outside of school, like sports.

He continued to play hockey by playing blind hockey, which is an adapted version of ice hockey for people who are visually impaired. Blake now plays for the US Blind Hockey Team! He is blown away by the opportunity to represent his country and help grow the sport to the Paralympic level. He also started working with the Anaheim Ducks to launch a local blind hockey program that will help impact others in the blind community. And if that weren't already enough, Blake has also continued to pursue his passion for mountain biking. He continues to traverse rocky descents by using a guide who rides in front of him and talks him through the trail.

He has grown a passion for using cameras to clearly capture the world around him, and he shares that perspective with others. Blake is now using his creative skills to create content on YouTube. In doing so, he's helping teach visually impaired people technology and playing a role in creating a more digitally accessible world.

Although it's been a challenging journey, Blake has overcome many obstacles and faced down stereotypes that even he used to believe about people with disabilities. He now considers it a privilege to be part of changing the narrative around disabilities. He uses his story to help change the way people see the disabled community. Blake recently said, "I want to show people that we all can adapt and overcome through the power of our perspective, passion, and the people we surround ourselves with." Blake Steinecke is a brilliant example of what it means to live life **Big, Bold, and Brave**. To learn more about his story and vision for the future, go to his website at adaptingsight.com or check out his YouTube channel, *Adapting Sight*.

Blake refused to give into the fear that came with losing his sight. Instead of shrinking and listening to all the things people said he couldn't do, he aggressively pursued new ways to conquer. Some people suffered brutal upbringings—abject poverty, losing parents to tragedy, or never knowing their family at all, to name just a few. Other children have had unspeakable things done to them. Physical and sexual abuse, relentless bullying, a lack of affection from others, or rejection in its various forms are common. Still, some of these children go on to conquer life as well. They refuse to *live* in fear. They choose to give their pain a purpose (more on that in a later chapter).

But others are marked for decades by their painful past. We all face unnatural fears at times—but for some these fears cause extreme reactions and rule them. Left unattended, these fears can cause significant stress and anxiety that affect the body, thought patterns, emotions, and the ability to rationally process a healthy response. Here's a short list of some possible situations where fear can become irrational and potentially destructive:

Fear of other races/ethnicities

People with different political views

Constant fear of dying or losing a loved one

Getting sick (known as illness anxiety disorder)

Being hurt emotionally or physically by another person

Being rejected by people

Losing a job/not finding a job

Failing at something

Public speaking (embarrassment)

Remaining or becoming financially poor

These fears all have one thing in common: They are based on a perception of what *could* happen *in the future*. Our natural fears help us become laser-focused to deal with immediate threats. It's time to *fight or flee!* Our brains won't allow us to get distracted by something less critical, because we want to *live*! These unnatural fears are all based on conjecture of a negative or destructive outcome that has yet to occur, and which MAY NEVER occur! These mental prophesies proudly instruct us to resist and barricade ourselves against risky situations.

In other words, some people will choose not to risk *anything* so risk doesn't have access to them. But guess what? That's a false reality! Folks, LIFE is a risky business. It has always been that way. It always *will be* that way. Since the pandemic hit in 2020, I have seen a tsunami of fear grip our planet. So have you. Use of fear mongering tactics to drive every social or political agenda you can dream of has become commonplace. And people are eating it up!

If you are going to live a Big, Bold, Brave life, breaking off your love affair with fear is essential.

Amárillys and I despise unnatural fears in every form. Please allow me to share how the impact of Gabriel's death sealed our perspective on how we approach this risky, dangerous, yet amazing and beautiful world we live in.

Returning to the trait of love—would you agree that love always wants what's best for a person? Could we agree that pure love is, in its very nature, selfless? I challenge you to find an ounce of love in pounding someone into submission with bad news, fear, tragedy, loss, pain, and hopelessness.

Let's get more specific. Allow me to inundate your life with news about violence. I am sure you would agree you will not feel *loved*. If you experience any emotion, it will likely be anger, hopelessness, anxiety, or even depression. If you need proof, watch the first fifteen minutes of just about any major news broadcast. Violent acts are always a "top story." Let's add heavy doses of financial crises, homelessness, unemployment rates, food shortages, racial tension, gender battles, and on and on.

I'm not saying those struggles don't exist or merit conversation. I am merely saying that love is not the driving force behind allowing these topics to be at the forefront of nightly news reports. Love does not drive the reason behind why it takes so long to find positive news when scrolling through stories on just about any media outlet on your phone. No, embedded in some of the "facts," you will find layers of fear being projected. Frankly, you don't even need to read articles in most cases. Headlines that immediately trigger fear are commonplace. It's become an art form. People who write catchy headlines get paid big bucks.

Fear is the true pandemic we face across the globe.

Fear fuels racism and just about any other social issue you can think of. Fear drives people to stay in careers or businesses they hate. Fear causes people to bury their dreams.

I have a friend who was the victim of a corporate layoff in 2021. Countless others have been too. Layoffs are certainly a scary thing. Maybe you've experienced one of them. No one wants to face a layoff. Most would prefer a promotion or to transition to a better job on our own terms. But it often doesn't happen that way. Many people go into a dark mental and emotional hole when their comfort is disrupted and their future is uncertain. Fear steamrolls in, and it doesn't ask permission. And fear, my friend, is the opposite of love and the mortal enemy of faith.

Fear has tried to beat us down many times. Amárillys' body has not responded well to pregnancy. I wrote in a previous chapter that Gabriel was born seven weeks early and weighed only 3lbs, 12oz. He spent four weeks in the hospital preparing for the outside world. He was delivered by C-section because Amárillys had preeclampsia. This condition causes elevated blood pressure that, if allowed to continue, can cause life-threatening consequences for both mommy and baby. You are put in the unenvious task of choosing life for mommy while also hoping you are making the right choice for the baby. But there is risk. Letting the disease run its course without medical intervention means choosing possible death for both.

When Gabriel was about two years old, Amárillys got pregnant again. We were very excited going into about the 12th week. Everything seemed great when she went in for a regularly scheduled sonogram. But they couldn't find the heartbeat. I understand that seems like a blunt transition. It was. In what seemed like an instant, we went from hopeful parents to the realization that she had suffered a miscarriage. It was a huge blow, and one I am painfully aware will touch many of you reading this book. I am so sorry for your loss. Experiencing a miscarriage can have long-term effects on our emotions. It also makes it very scary to consider another pregnancy and can cause anxiety if you do get pregnant again.

We were advised by our doctor to wait at least six months before trying again. We decided to leave it up to divine providence. Within a couple of months, we were pregnant with Joel. We fought through the fear of suffering another loss and did everything in our power to keep Amárillys healthy. Well, healthy aside from indulging in all her Taco Bell cravings! Being the great husband I was, I took a *run to the border* every time the craving hit. I even ate with her—so much that I gained twenty pounds while she carried Joel! He would reach full term with just the normal discomforts of pregnancy. When we arrived at the hospital, we anticipated a natural delivery. She tried her best, but after twelve hours of labor her dilation halted at 4 cm. We proceeded with a C-section.

The anesthesiologist had difficulty getting the epidural in the right spot. Just before they were about to make the incision, Amárillys still had feeling from the waist down. It was puzzling for the doctors and scary for us! After some moments of anxiety, they decided she would have to be put completely under anesthesia. I was not allowed in the room, so I impatiently waited until I was called upon. Though it felt agonizingly long to me, the C-section was completed quickly. A nurse came and escorted me into the room where Joel was being cleaned up, and I got to hold him for the first time. I experienced such overwhelming joy—Joel was healthy and strong. Finally, I could relax! But then, suddenly, I got called back into the recovery room where they were trying to revive Amárillys from the anesthesia.

She was struggling to wake up. And while the staff remained calm and professional, they were clearly alarmed. The anesthesiologist asked me to help by not letting her fall asleep and continuing to have a conversation with her. This went on for some time. She kept fading, and I kept gently telling her she needed to stay awake. The fear of losing Amárillys was a very real threat. I did my best to stay calm and pray for her recovery, but inside I was terrified. Eventually she began to fully recover from the effects, and we were out of the danger zone. Amárillys and Joel would leave the hospital healthy and whole. We agreed we were done having children! But time changes things, and five years later we tried to get pregnant one last time.

When our youngest son Liam was in the womb, the first six months were relatively smooth. We believed he would reach full term. Our middle son Joel had gone full term, so we thought Amárillys was past the threat of a recurrence of the disease. All was going well. That is, until I decided to take a trip.

We had accepted a position near Seattle, and for the first six weeks we had hopped between homes hosted by church members and staff. We moved seven times in total during those six weeks before some friends graciously offered to let us use their home for an entire year. They had moved to another city and were not ready to sell yet. We took care of the house, paid the utilities, and lived out of what we had packed in our suitcases while we tried to sell our home back in Louisiana.

This was in 2008-09 during the infamous housing crisis. To make matters worse, Southeast Louisiana had not only suffered from Hurricane Katrina, but Hurricane Gustav had recently hit the region as well. Getting a home insured was expensive—if you could even find a company to insure it. During the span of an entire year, only one home sold in our area. An attempt at selling our home via short sale was denied by the bank after we'd waited on an answer for eight months. We could no longer afford to pay the mortgage. So, our house was put up for auction by the local sheriff on *three* different occasions! Miraculously, the sheriff would take it back off without telling us why. The house just sat, fully staged with all of our stuff.

It was a very challenging season. We'd gone far too long living without our possessions, and we needed stability. We made the decision to have movers bring all our furniture and belongings to Washington so we could find a permanent place to live.

The morning of my trip, Amárillys wasn't feeling well. She was slightly swollen, but we felt she would be fine until I got back. I hopped on a plane bound for New Orleans with a crisp plan in place to pack and help the movers load over the next few days, then return home to wait for the big move into a new home. There was no direct flight to New Orleans from Seattle, so it took me one connection in Dallas and eight hours of total travel to arrive at Louis Armstrong International Airport. I called her as soon as I got in my rental car.

In those eight hours, Amárillys' situation had gone from what seemed manageable to horribly wrong. She informed me her blood pressure had spiked to a scary 200+ over 100+! She was already at the hospital, where she received some medication to prevent seizures and took some additional tests. I told her I'd call back after I purchased some packing supplies. I hadn't even arrived at our house yet!

I finished my Walmart run and called her as soon as I got to the house. Her condition had worsened, and they were transferring her to a special regional NICU unit in Tacoma! In a matter of hours, we went from thinking everything was good to there being a real threat her and Liam's lives were in danger. She'd changed hospitals to meet with a doctor she had never met, AND I was in freaking Louisiana! They gave her a steroid injection in hopes they could buy Liam another 48 hours and give him a better chance at survival after a C-section to save her life. Her preeclampsia had escalated into HELLP Syndrome, an advanced stage of preeclampsia that was causing her major internal organs to shut down. I had arrived in New Orleans around 8:30 p.m. and was back on a return flight by 7:00 a.m. the next morning. I had to get home!

Thank God, I was able to get to the hospital by late afternoon. We rode out the next day together, and she made it through the 48 hours. The doctor came in to tell us they had done their best to stall, but now she needed the C-section ASAP, or she was going to die. His bedside manner was better than those choice of words—I'm just giving you the literal implications we faced.

Liam was at twenty-seven weeks of development, a full thirteen weeks shy of the forty-week benchmark and ten short of what is considered premature at thirty-seven weeks. I was allowed in the operating room and was positioned behind Amárillys' head. This was strategic, as I was in perfect position to comfort her while the vantage point guarded me from viewing the C-section procedure.

The surgery did not go smoothly. At one point, her body was mercilessly jerked around as they were having a difficult time safely removing Liam from the womb. The procedure was relatively quick, but it felt like everything was in slow motion. Finally, Liam was pulled out and quickly cleaned off before being rushed into the NICU unit. He needed to be placed in a high-tech incubator to have a chance at survival. Liam was officially born three months early at a whopping 1lb, 14oz! That is not a typo. At that size, he resembled what a malnourished E.T. would have looked like at birth. It was shocking. I was asked to follow the nurse with Liam and leave Amárillys in the surgery room. A feeling I will never forget.

I knew she had the best care possible, but I was whisked out before seeing any evidence that she was okay. Once again, I had to resist fear and choose thoughts of *life*. Medically speaking, Liam needed me more in that moment than she did. One of the immediate challenges facing an extremely premature baby is that they do not benefit from skin-to-skin bonding with the mother. I was stationed outside Liam's incubator, meaning I could gently touch him through plastic gloves that allow you to reach inside of the protective unit. I was also commissioned to keep talking to him so he could hear my voice. It was important to comfort him in the wake of being jolted into isolation. He was hooked up to several machines that helped his lungs, heart, brain, and other vital organs finish developing (since they could no longer do so within the womb). The thought that he would be in this contraption for up to three months was too much to take in. All we could do was take it one day at a time.

Speaking life over your child in this situation is not terribly heroic, awe-inspiring, or even admirable. Motivated by love, you will fight to the death to save or protect your child. You will not let fear overtake you and convince you to quit! There is a chorus of competing voices trying to convince you things won't end well, and they are demonic and relentless in nature.

One such voice liked to mock us through a device designed to measure what doctors and nurses commonly refer to as *Brady* episodes.

Liam was born so early that his brain was still learning to communicate with his lungs. In this stage of development, the baby forgets to breathe, which of course is lethal. When the equipment detects that the baby has gone too long between breaths, a loud bell starts ringing. This is an early warning system for the staff to be aware that intervention may be necessary to help the baby start breathing again. It can be a short waiting game of only fifteen seconds before the episode is typically corrected by gently touching parts of the body to remind the baby to breathe. However, the baby often does not immediately respond, and the beeps from the monitor just keep repeating until he or she starts breathing again. The enemy would try to use the sound of the bell as an opportune moment to strike fear into our hearts. It was that little voice trying to tell us Liam would die. How often did we endure these bells, you ask? Since these episodes happen dozens of times per day—and most premature babies stop having apnea and bradycardia (the technical terms) when they reach thirty-six or thirty-seven weeks—the answer is way too often and for far too long!

Fearing *less* was paramount to keeping our sanity. We had faith God would intervene and that He had an army praying with us. The love of God and those around us were a huge factor for us to deflect fear and believe in the best. The heart-wrenching reality was that many parents in that unit had no source of faith or hope that their baby would be coming out of the NICU alive. You could see it on their faces and body language. Many times, we wanted to reach out and say something to give them hope. Unfortunately, a policy was in place where you were not allowed to engage other people in the NICU to give them privacy. In some cases, babies did not have anyone coming to visit them for days or weeks! There could have been a variety of reasons for this out of the parents' control. And there were additional protocols in place for health measures.

Liam was born during the peak of the H1N1 virus outbreak. Policy dictated that only the birth parents could visit the NICU. That's right, for what would end up being two and a half months, Amárillys and I were the only ones allowed in the NICU with Liam because of the fear of a virus spreading. Sound familiar? No grandparents, aunts or uncles, or close friends. Even Liam's older brothers never laid eyes on him until his release from the hospital. It was an incredibly difficult season that required some complicated time management. We had to make sure Gabriel and Joel were taken care of and ensure Liam was visited enough.

We constantly felt like we were failing in both aspects! We were away from the boys too often and never with Liam enough. A few times, we even had to have Gabriel and Joel sit in the waiting room with one of us for hours. That's really tough for an eight- and five-year-old child. They handled it well beyond their years, but it really sucked! We also still had jobs, and the commute to the hospital was a thirty-five-minute trip *one way*. It was reasonable to understand how there were likely single moms or working parents who simply could not visit the NICU often under such conditions. The pain and hopelessness we saw on the faces of some parents was heartbreaking. Honoring the rules, we silently spoke life over the parents and their babies.

What does it look like to speak life in challenging situations? I mentioned before that fear thrives in environments lacking love.

A posture of love gives you the fuel to speak life into any circumstance. This doesn't mean you disregard information or deny that conditions are unfavorable. However, love does deny fear, worry, and hopelessness the opportunity to control you.

I consider fear, worry, and hopelessness to be wicked cousins. They'll conspire to convince you that things are going to go against you. If you allow them, you'll experience the emotions and crippling effects of a *death* mentality, whether the wicked prophecy ever actually materializes or not. Meanwhile, with love as a catalyst you can experience *life* even in the direst of situations. You get to choose which you invite to stay—fear or love. One of the greatest enemies of love can be anger, especially if it is powered by the unwillingness to forgive. More on that later.

Once Liam was released from the hospital, we still faced two years of specialty doctors' visits and the *possible* reality of him developing lifelong disabilities, or worse. We remained aware of the difficulties described to us by well-meaning doctors, nurses, and even parents with similar stories. We elevated our faith in God over the fear of a "what if?" We did not entertain fear, worry, or hopelessness even though they kept knocking at our door. Now, this doesn't mean we never looked through the peephole—we just refused to open the door and let fear and its companions live with us.

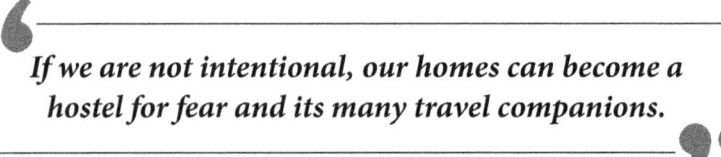

> *If we are not intentional, our homes can become a hostel for fear and its many travel companions.*

Liam thrived from the moment he left the hospital. As I write this, our son—who arrived home wrapped in a swaddle, the size of a Chipotle burrito—is almost thirteen years old and killing it in middle school. He is strong-willed and strong physically. He has a brilliant mind and tremendous communication skills. He recently earned his first-degree black belt in Taekwondo. Consequently, we have experienced abundant life throughout this journey with Liam. Here's something that may surprise you. In those hours before we knew Gabriel had passed away, we spoke life into the atmosphere. Did we experience the same result? No and *yes!*

Let me explain. We did not get the answer we wanted regarding Gabriel's crash. The crushing pain of him not coming home again was VERY real, and it still is. We miss him every day, and we wish our story had another narrative. However, as bizarre as this may sound to you, our faith assures us we will see him again. He is not dead. He is more alive than ever, and we firmly believe he has continued an amazing journey and mission with God that is beyond our ability to fully comprehend. Even with his physical death on this planet, we have chosen *life* for our future. In these radically contrasting stories with Gabriel and Liam, we have spoken life through the medium of love, and life is exactly what we have received more of. It's not perfect or how we always draw it up, but it is a journey full of love and life, nonetheless. You have that same choice.

And now, with Gabriel having left this Earth nearly three years ago, we carry his love and life in our hearts, thoughts, and actions. We refuse to let fear dictate our decisions. That is how **Big, Bold, Brave** humans live! I believe learning to make courageous decisions is ground zero. (We'll cover what I mean by that in the next chapter.)

Chapter 8 Reflection

List your greatest fears. (Have a simple chart distinguishing from natural and unnatural fears.) I will give a few of my own as examples:

Natural	Unnatural
Bears!	Being Rejected
Drowning	Facing another personal tragedy
A gun pointed at me	Starting a business

CHAPTER 9
COURAGEOUS DECISIONS

SOMETIMES FEAR DOESN'T creep in, it runs down the track like a runaway freight train—especially if you listen to all the voices spewing doom and gloom these days. Scary news is everywhere. Why? Is it because there are more negative things going on in the world? Because hopeful stories are hard to find? Nope! That is not why. I discussed this in the previous chapter. Human nature has proven to be more attracted to fear or negative stories. The media learned decades ago that if they wanted to sell newspapers, accumulate airtime to advertise on television, and now utilize the influence of social media, they would have to feed fear more than love and hope. As they say, "If it bleeds, it leads." Fear sells. If we are going to divorce ourselves from the world's love affair with fear, doing so will require making courageous decisions motivated by a love for yourself and other humans.

As I said, the opposite of fear is *love*. Notice I didn't say the opposite of fear is faith? Let me explain. In the ancient text of the Bible, there is a verse that says *perfect love casts out all fear*. It does not say perfect *faith* casts out all fear. Love is a powerful force. Love contains within it a powerful mixture of life-breathing characteristics, which I broke down earlier in the book: love, joy, peace, patience, kindness, goodness, faithfulness, gentleness, and self-control. Each have the potential to radically change your perspective. Change your perspective, change your life, AND change the lives of others! Fear is an enemy of love and faith because it is void of these life-breathing traits. Fear causes you to have "stinking" thinking of various kinds. Some damage your personal life. Others wreak havoc over all of humanity and often create deep wounds and violent responses.

Racism is perhaps one of the oldest and most disgusting human expressions of fear. It can breed deep hatred toward other human beings instead of embracing the beauty of the diversity in which humans were created. The world is filled with those who use fear of other races to create division, prejudice, and injustice towards our fellow man. The world needs more heroes to rise up in love and demolish these destructive mindsets. Daryl Davis has been one of those heroes for over forty years. Daryl has graciously given me permission to share some of his story.

Daryl Davis is an international recording artist, actor, and leader of The Daryl Davis Band. He's considered one of the greatest blues boogie-woogie and rock 'n' roll pianists of all time, having played with The Legendary Blues Band (formerly the Muddy Waters band) and Chuck Berry. As an actor, Daryl has received rave reviews for his stage role in William Saroyan's *The Time of Your Life*. Daryl has done film and television and even had a role in the critically acclaimed five-year HBO television series, *The Wire*.

However, his greatest contribution to the world and the legacy he has forged came in a very different form. Daryl experienced racism firsthand as a young boy. During the mid-eighties, Davis decided he wanted to interview Klan members and write a book on the subject. Why? As he said, to answer the "question in my head from the age of ten: 'Why do you hate me when you know nothing about me?' That question had never been answered from my youth."

His first interview was with Roger Kelly, at that time a KKK Grand Wizard. Daryl set up a meeting through his white secretary. She was instructed not to mention that he was a black man, only that he was writing a book on the Klan. The meeting was intense. Daryl went out of his way to *listen* to Roger Kelly. He spent years building trust between them and laying the foundation of what became a friendship. They broke bread at each other's tables. They welcomed each other into their homes. Davis even went as far as attending Klan rallies as a guest of Kelly.

Most importantly, Davis cultivated an atmosphere of listening. He didn't hate Kelly because Kelly hated him. Instead, he listened to Roger Kelly. Eventually, Kelly started listening to him. This led to the two realizing they had far more in common than not. In the end, Kelly denounced his ties to the KKK and handed his hood and robe to Daryl Davis. In total, Davis has now seen over 200 Klan members walk away from the KKK and hand over their robes and hoods to him.

As a race relations expert, Daryl has received acclaim for both his book and documentary—*Klan-Destine Relationships*, and *Accidental Courtesy*, respectively—from many respected sources including CNN, NBC, Good Morning America, TLC, NPR, The Washington Post, and others. He is also the recipient of numerous awards including the Elliott-Black Award, the MLK Award, the Bridge Builder Award, and many others. Filled with exciting encounters and amusing anecdotes, Daryl's impassioned lectures leave an audience feeling empowered to confront their own prejudices and overcome their fears. Daryl is a world changer replacing fear-driven hate with love. Because love conquers fear ... every time! Daryl Davis lives his life, **Big, Bold, and Brave!**

Daryl's powerful perspective on life and his ability to enact change is not an exception to the rule. His example is vivid proof that what we think and believe are strong indicators of what we can experience in life and the influence we can have. Science is proving it! We've gathered great evidence in the last decade from the study of the mind (neuroscience and its various forms) and human psychology. This evidence suggests that what we think and believe about ourselves, and our opportunities, will ultimately dictate the results we get in life and affect our physical and mental health.

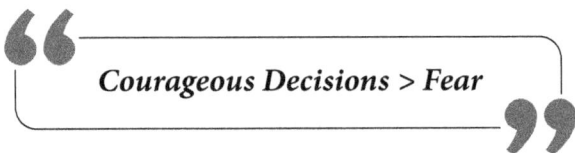

Courageous Decisions > Fear

How do you start beating fear? Make one courageous decision, then act on it! Despite losing his eyesight, Blake Steinecke has stacked courageous decisions that have allowed him to serve others and have great personal success. Daryl Davis has made repeated courageous decisions and has turned enemies into friends. Every inch of personal growth and transformation is birthed with a courageous decision. Every pound lost, every healthy relationship, every new friend, every sound investment, every new business thrust into existence was birthed by a courageous decision.

A courageous decision often begins the process of rewiring your brain and the way you think about change, fear, and risk. That first step creates the ability in you to make a series of powerful decisions. When acted upon, these decisions can radically transform your life! The scary thing is NOT choosing to make a courageous decision. Doing so keeps you stuck in a holding pattern or creates room for a downward spiral.

Prior to Gabriel's accident, we were often asked if we worried that something bad could happen. Worry, of course, is one of the pathetic cousins of fear. Worry's mission is to predict and experience the worst possible outcome before it happens. That said, it was a legitimate question. And the answer was a resounding, "Yes!" I believe every parent whose teenage son or daughter is driving a car alone for the first (and probably thousandth) time has had to fight the enemy of worry. Heck, worry may have knocked on your door when your child first attempted to ride a bike or skateboard! Amárillys may feel slightly different, but I personally had to fight off more worry when Gabriel got in his car than when he was flying. I had a couple of very practical reasons. One was that I felt the odds of him being in a crash driving around our congested and sometimes chaotic highways in the Dallas Metroplex were riskier than him crashing a plane. Second, like many teenagers, Gabriel could be very casual with his attention while driving a car, and he occasionally drove too fast. In contrast, he was incredibly focused and intense about safety precautions when he was flying a plane.

Gabriel discovered his passion for flying at eight years old, when he got an opportunity to fly in a private aircraft with his Uncle Dan. He caught the proverbial bug, and the rest was history! When he was sixteen and had the opportunity to start flight training, Amárillys and I had two options. We made a courageous decision to accept the dangers and allow him to chase his dream of becoming a pilot, instead of giving into the "what-ifs?" of worry and fear and deny him the chance. One choice kills life before it can get off the ground. The other grants permission to lead an adventurous life. We willingly and intentionally chose the latter. The risk was real, and we had moments where worry or fear brushed us.

So, the question isn't "Will we ever get touched by worry or fear?" The question is "Will we allow those wicked cousins to dictate our life?" You can't always avoid being touched by worry or fear, but you can harness the power to keep it from ruling your life.

One of the saddest things I have witnessed in the post-pandemic world is the way fear has caused so many people to go into seclusion or stop living their normal lives. There are some more extreme examples: there are families that won't visit a grandparent in person or those who have intentionally stayed away to avoid *possibly* getting sick and *possibly* dying for the last two years! It's tragic. Human connection is the most valuable aspect of being alive. It's been hard for my family to understand. Our reasoning is quite simple and came at great cost.

We suffered one of the greatest losses imaginable on this side of eternity. Gabriel's death signifies an outcome of risk taking we hoped to never face. Still, we refuse to create a revisionist history of accepting those risks just because our story took a turn we didn't plan for. We accepted those risks so Gabriel could pursue and realize his dream of being a pilot. He achieved it. We have no regrets. That might puzzle some readers, which I understand. It's all about perspective. We have no regrets because we held nothing back in allowing him to chase his dream. We *loved* him too much not to.

> *The veil between this life and eternity is razor-thin. And so is the veil between merely existing and chasing your dreams!*

To be clear, just under eighteen years was not nearly long enough with him. He wasn't the only person who had dreams and goals for his tomorrow. We had dreams of him becoming a commercial pilot and the CEO of a company someday (partly because he would never be happy answering to a boss)! We dreamed of his future bride, his grandchildren (and spoiling the fire out of them), and his accomplishments. We want him back every day, just not at the expense of him not being able to live his life the way *he* wanted. Yes, I really do feel that way. He was a wild stallion, and he lived more in his short seventeen years than many do in a lifetime.

Many have mundane lives. They are literally the *walking dead*. Trudging through life, going through the motions. Playing it safe by risking nothing at all. Before you accuse me of being insensitive, allow me to say one more thing. The way Gabriel lived life revealed something about me that I had ignored for far too long. In many ways, *I* was one of the walking dead. I became jealous of his zest for life, his risk taking, and the way he treated life as one prolonged adventure rather than a chore. We also had his two younger brothers to consider. Conceding to fear and risk in areas of *my* life had to stop, immediately. It's been necessary to our pursuit of living **Big, Bold, and Brave**. I will share some more principles later to help you make the shift away from fear.

I'm aware I might have made some of you angry just now. I'm okay with that. As humans, we often get angry about remarks directed at us personally because we know truth is imbedded in them. I get most upset with my wife when she says something about me that I don't *want* to be true. I typically react with denial and defensiveness. To grow and become a more powerful version of myself, I had to embrace the truth of my deficiency. At the very least, I hope you can understand why certain people (like me) refuse to ingest all the fear that has been unleashed in the world—because we *despise all fear* that causes us to miss out on our best life.

As I write this, it's been almost three years since that fateful day. Though we didn't sign up for this, we have learned more about the grieving process and what it means to believe that God is good no matter the circumstance. The scriptures make it quite clear: "In this world, you *will* have *tribulation.*" Our promise from God stops short of a guarantee that we will not suffer in this broken world. In fact, it is assured we *will* suffer. It won't look or even feel the same for everyone, but eventually everyone will face tribulation. If you are not familiar with this word, it is from the Greek word *"thlip'-sis,"* which means "pressure" (literally or figuratively), afflicted, anguished, burdened, persecuted, and troubled. The *Encyclopedia of Biblical Words* defines it as "the idea of great emotional or spiritual stress that can be caused by external or internal pressure." Pressure is a stark reality, and no one knows what it feels like more than Jesus.

Read about His very personal experience in the Garden of Gethsemane prior to suffering on the cross, a tribulation He passionately endured for all of humanity. Case closed. This is also why we can be assured that God knows exactly how to carry us through our pain and times of extreme disappointment. He helps us fear *less* and make courageous decisions. I repeat, if you are going to live a **Big, Bold, and Brave** lifestyle, you must break off your love affair with fear! Whatever form of fear is stealing from your life today, make a courageous decision to defeat it!

Chapter 9 Reflection

5-Step Guide to Making Courageous Decisions

1. Decide what courageous decision needs to be made.

2. Determine what action is necessary to execute the decision.

3. Establish a definitive timeline in which you will execute the decision. The sooner the better!

4. Tell someone trustworthy about the decision—someone you know will hold you accountable to follow through.

5. After you have executed fully on this courageous decision, write down at least five more courageous decisions you need to make! By stacking courageous decisions, each subsequent decision gets easier. This will CHANGE YOUR LIFE!

Here's a few courageous decisions you can consider starting with:

Call or visit someone you need to forgive or whom you need to ask for forgiveness.

Update your resume and start searching for the career you really want!

Start a business within the next 30 days ... it's been done before!

If you have been struggling with depression, anxiety, or mental illness on your own, let someone into your circle within the next 24 hours.

Initiate the difficult conversation that is long overdue with your spouse, child, boss, co-worker, etc.

Chapter 10
Giving Pain a Purpose

B**ig, Bold, and Brave**—it started as our life mantra. It was the *go-to* phrase to keep breathing, keep stepping, keep loving, and keep dreaming. Early in the grieving process, it became the catalyst for a metamorphosis into something bigger. It became my clarion call. Whenever pain would try to take me down a road of sadness and hopelessness, I would think about the way Gabriel lived. I would remember how tenacious he was about reaching his goal of being a licensed pilot. Nothing could stop him. He *knew* he was going to be a pilot.

Gabriel got his Student Pilot's License and flew solo at sixteen—before he had received a driver's license! But before he could fly solo, he had to pass medical and written exams. If you've ever seen the manual a hopeful pilot must study from, you know it's an intimidating sight. You could use the manual as a jack to change your car tires! The test consists of the following topics: Regulations, Accident Reporting, Performance Charts, Radio Communications, Weather, Safe and Efficient Operations, Density Altitude Performance, Weight and Balance, Aerodynamics, Powerplants and Aircraft Systems, Stalls and Spins, Aeronautical Decision-Making (ADM), and Preflight Actions. My head is spinning just typing all that! I remember Amárillys helped

Gabriel prepare for the exam during his last couple weeks of studying. By help, I mean she quizzed him by reading possible questions. I laugh even now thinking about her describing the study sessions: "It was hard to even *read* the questions!"

The day Amárillys and I watched his first solo flight was quite an experience. Seeing him go up without his Flight Instructor invoked conflicting feelings: great pride in his hard work and courage as he ascended, but then butterflies in our stomach and anxiety as he descended to land. The look on his face when he got out of the little Cessna, nicknamed 35Ugly (a combo of the aircrafts tail number and appearance), was priceless. The joy he exuded outweighed our fears. The day ended with an aviation club tradition of tearing the back of his Tango 31 Aero Clube t-shirt. His flight instructor then wrote the date of the solo and signed the remaining back of the shirt. We have it on video, which we love watching to this day. I also kept the shirt as a symbol of courage.

He had a few more hurdles left to jump. A prospective private pilot must also complete a minimum of forty hours of flight training. This includes day, night, and cross-country flying, and other types of flight requirements and maneuvers. The last step to earning a Private Pilot's License is the check ride. During a check ride, you're required to take two tests with an FAA-approved examiner. First is an oral examination where you're quizzed extensively on your knowledge of everything from aircraft systems to rules and regulations. Once he passed that portion, he had to fly the airplane and demonstrate what he'd learned. This final step causes the greatest angst in most pilots. It's intense, and you must have the answers memorized, ready to answer on the fly (pun intended) as the instructor peppers you with questions. Gabriel was no exception. We know a few pilots who failed this step the first time (some failed multiple times). Besides the disappointment of failing, you must pay the fee (a few hundred dollars) to retest each time. But Gabriel was prepared, and he passed with flying colors. (I know, another pun, but it fits!)

You might be wondering, "What does this part of his story have to do with giving your pain a purpose?" I'm glad you asked. The answer is nothing *and everything*. In previous chapters, I discussed our family's disdain for giving in to fear. Now I want to talk about how to turn a great loss or disappointment into a catalyst. Reminiscing about the way Gabriel pursued his passions became a source of inspiration for me. He was supposed to outlive me. Amárillys and I would eventually pass the torch. Instead, our family carries *his* torch.

Several months into our new journey, I began toying with the idea of getting a tattoo. I know some of you are cringing, while others are thinking how cool that is. I was fifty-four years old and did not have any tattoos. See, I'd followed a two-week rule I had implemented in my twenties: every time I considered getting a tattoo, I would sit on the idea for two weeks and see if I was still excited about it. Up to that point in my life, I never had a design in mind that withstood the two-week test. I know tattoos are an expression of art for some people and that not every tattoo has a meaningful story behind it, but *I* needed a compelling reason. If I got a tattoo, it had to tell a story that inspired me and those who ask about it.

The phrase **Big, Bold, and Brave** kept echoing in my mind. It's how *we* wanted to live the rest of our lives. I worked for months on a design to illustrate that motto. Here's what I came up with.

The design is in black ink and includes a band around my forearm, symbolizing the circle of life. The band is not a smooth circle—the outer edges have a jagged tribal appearance that represents family. The band was created to have a negative space revealing the words Big Bold Brave. (A negative space tattoo is where the ink is placed in such a way that the untouched skin creates a design or message.)

As the band comes around the back of my forearm towards the front, it does not complete a circle. Instead, it breaks off and runs down my forearm. This element reveals that the normal circle of life did not complete, as we naturally expected to outlive our son. At the break, the band turns into a dotted line to resemble a jet plane's contrails (the white trail you see in the sky behind a plane).

Continuing down my arm, just shy of my wrist, the contrails come out of the exhaust of a F-22 Raptor Fighter Jet. Gabriel did not fly military jets, he flew Cessna's. But I chose the F-22 because it spoke to his personality. He was a fighter from the day he was born seven weeks prematurely! An F-22 also has a pointed nose that mimics an arrowhead. This is a tip to a scripture in the Bible that says *children are like a quiver full of arrows* (Psalm 127).

The less obvious aspect of the tattoo is why the jet is flying *down* my arm instead of up. One thing that got me through the shock and awe faze of grieving was the process of lifting my arms in gratefulness and worshipping God. I wrote about the most intense occasion I experienced in Chapter 5. It brought me peace back then, and it still does whenever I sense a darkness wanting to fall over me. When you look at my tattoo when I am in this posture, the jet is flying straight up into the heavens. It's a stark reminder of where my true help comes from and of Gabriel's current residence. When you put this all together, our story is told. The tattoo is also a vivid nudge to choose to live **Big, Bold, and Brave** *every day*. Some days, that nudge is more like a shove!

In May 2020, I was ready to bring this vision to life. I chose a tattoo shop recommended by a friend. A tattoo artist greeted me in the lobby, and I described to her what I wanted done. She had tattoos from head to toe and hair dyed pink. Her demeanor was a little gruff. I figured she must've created many tattoos to remember a loved one during her career. I didn't expect a reaction to my design. But when I finished the explanation of the design, I was caught off guard as she began to weep. She was deeply moved by the story. She was especially moved that the message of my tattoo was not a memorial to someone who'd died—it was a message of love, family, and the promise of a glorious reunion that will take place. She gathered her emotions and told me she was the wrong person to ink the tattoo, but she knew the perfect artist for the job.

She stepped into the back of the shop and returned with another artist. Out came James, a super chill dude exuding kindness like it was a force field surrounding him. Like the other artist, he had numerous tattoos. He also had long salt-and-pepper hair and a matching beard at the time. I explained my vision, and he got excited. It turned out James was known in the tattoo world by another name: the Tattoo Reverend! He's been inking tattoos for many years and shares the story of his love for Jesus with everyone sitting in his chair. We quickly became friends.

I was prepared for *some* pain. I was convinced this sort of pain couldn't compare to the pain of losing my son. Heck, this sort of pain was *nothing*. I expected to cruise through the process. And I did for a couple of hours. But during the last thirty minutes, I almost had to tap out for a break. Just when I was about to whine—I mean, uh, ask for a break—James announced he was finished. Getting the tattoo was a token gesture in beginning to give my pain a purpose. After that, more significant forms of doing so began to unfold.

I can't talk about how to give your pain a purpose without circling back to the concept of choosing life over death. If you tend to look through the lens of death—meaning you focus on what you lost and how you lost it—you are sealing that part of your journey in a grave in your mind. Giving your pain a purpose takes courage. It will be difficult. You will likely be in a constant battle against fear. And remember, fear is the opposite of love.

Giving your pain a purpose, through the filter of love, changes everything.

The tattoo was just a start. Let me tie Gabriel's journey back in. I will state the obvious. He *died* flying a plane, that's a *fact*. As I said, we've avoided creating a revisionist history of his story. We don't regret his becoming a pilot. Flying was his *passion*. He was more at home in the air than on the ground.

GIVING PAIN A PURPOSE

The same is true for anyone who relentlessly pursues their passions. I can't imagine wanting to ascend Mount Everest, but some people do and have died trying. I'm not interested in putting on a wingsuit (the suit that makes you look like a flying squirrel) and jumping off a cliff thousands of feet above the ground. I do not share Gabriel's passion to become a pilot. I do, however, have a passion to carry his legacy forward and inspire others through his story. That includes his passion for aviation.

This has been paramount for me in confronting how I can suffer the pain of his loss simultaneously while embracing a hope for the future. Many people bury their pain in a futile attempt to forget. They may fool themselves, but their soul doesn't forget. Others wear their pain as an identity and are bound by it. I believe there is a healthier perspective.

> *To bury the pain of losing my son invalidates the great love we still share.*
> *To allow the pain to imprison me would negate the legacy he left inside of me. I embrace the pain. I use it as a catalyst.*

The first dream I had for giving pain a purpose was to establish a scholarship in Gabriel's name that would benefit another young person with a passion for aviation. Gabriel's path to becoming a licensed pilot was not typical. When he entered high school, he was certain he would become a pilot, he just didn't know how it would happen. Neither did we. Anyone who has ever attempted to become a pilot is aware of how expensive it is. The cost of flight training varies widely. A private pilot certificate can cost between $4,000 and $15,000 (or more). This price depends on the location, type of airplane used, type of flight school, instructor experience, and the pace at which a student can learn. We just didn't have a budget for that on my salary.

Gabriel didn't let that deter him. He landed a $1,000 scholarship to help with the cost. As I've mentioned, he also joined a local aviation club called Tango Thirty One Aero Club. This would become the single most important move that would ultimately allow him to fulfill his dream of flying.

Tango Thirty One Aero Clube is a 501(c)3 non-profit organization founded by Kevin Lacey. Kevin is a legend to many in the private sector of aviation. He gained fame while starring in a television show called *Airplane Repo*, which you can still watch on The Discovery Channel. Kevin repos every kind of plane you can imagine! He's also passionate about young people interested in aviation. He started the club to give teenagers an opportunity to learn about aviation, get hands-on training for how to restore and maintain aircraft, and to give those interested in becoming a pilot a chance to fly. Through his many connections in the aviation field, he has been able to secure funding and flight training at virtually no cost to the students. The fee to be a part of the club is only $50 a year. He has agreements in place with flight instructors that volunteer their time. Students that fly can also purchase fuel at cost.

The students invest heavily in *sweat equity*. Prospective pilots must earn their airtime. The Clube members participate in aircraft maintenance, repairs, and flight operations. Several members have earned FAA Certificates for Private Pilot and Airframe & Powerplant Mechanics. The Clube is based out of Aero Country Airport in McKinney, Texas, and is identified by the FAA as T31. It's an amazing organization. If you would like to support students who are pursuing aviation, I hope you consider making a tax-deductible donation. You can find out more about the Clube by going to their website, t31aeroclube.com. Kevin and T31 have been an incredible source of blessing to us, and we consider him and the students family. Promoting this club is another way I give my pain a purpose.

In the end, the $1,000 scholarship Gabriel was awarded paid for all his fuel in flight training, plus other ancillary costs. The only out-ofpocket expense we had was his certificate exam, which only cost a few hundred dollars. There are only a couple of clubs like this in the country, and Gabriel's scholarship went further than we could have ever imagined. I wanted to do the same for someone else.

Before I could even hatch my plans to establish a scholarship, I was contacted by an organization called Relay: Heroes Today Leaders Tomorrow. The organization's founder and current executive director is our dear friend, Lottia Fredo. Relay Heroes was established in part out of a growing passion for helping individuals become college-ready and financially literate, and to assist families and individuals in their overall sustainability goals. The organization's goal is to connect individuals and families to resources that enhance their educational experience and opportunities. Lottia had met with Gabriel in person to help him explore various paths to his continued education. Their interaction created a lasting connection between the two of them. Relay Heroes sponsors one scholarship each year for both the spring and fall semesters in the name of a "hero." Lottia, in agreement with the board of directors, asked if we would be willing to allow them to present one in honor of Gabriel. We could even help name it and establish the application criteria. Another cool thing was the amount of this scholarship: $1,000! The same amount Gabriel had earned! Amárillys and I cried and of course said YES! We are forever grateful to Relay Heroes. It would be the first scholarship, but not the last.

I'm currently in the process of establishing a non-profit foundation to fund and manage an annual scholarship in Gabriel's name for a student lacking the financial means to pursue a career in aviation. The goal is $50,000 a year. At the time of writing this book, I was already contacted by an organization that has committed $1,000 a year towards the scholarship indefinitely. The scholarship is another step in giving my pain a purpose. It will bring *life* to a special individual and perpetuate the story of how Gabriel lived.

Giving our pain a purpose does not eliminate the pain. It is not meant to be a replacement for grieving or feeling the sting of

Gabriel's absence. We grieve in some measure every birthday, holiday, graduation, and even at times when a plane flies overhead or ordering a meal he would have liked. Triggers can hit at any time. They don't ask for permission to enter our minds or assault our hearts. I am at complete peace with that. The pain will never completely go away, nor do I want it to. It visits because of the deep love I have for Gabriel and the gaping hole that was left on this side of eternity, which only he can fill. But giving the pain a purpose *does* fend off that pain from turning into a sense of despair or believing his legacy died with him.

The pain of loss or disappointment may come from a very different source for you. You may have lost a loved one under different circumstances. You may have lost a business you spent your life building. You may have lost your career due to the way the world has responded to the pandemic. Many have suffered because of the effects of divorce (I can relate to that too). I am not implying that the trauma from such losses is easy to extinguish or that one simple action will change your life overnight. The truth is, you only have two choices when faced with the pain of loss or disappointment. You can learn to thrive despite the pain, or you can let it dictate your life. It can be a catalyst or a roadblock, an inspiration or hope killer.

Allow me to share with you two powerful examples of how your pain can become a catalyst to serve others.

Colby and Caroline Harries

Colby and Caroline Harries took their marriage vows in 2011. Their life together began like most couples—with hopes, dreams, and desires for a promising future. For the Harries, that included having children. Shortly after they married, they decided to have some baseline tests done to gauge their ability to get pregnant and have a baby. They knew they were ready and wanted to start a family soon. In a painful moment, their tests revealed they would never have biological children. The report was devastating.

After arriving home from the appointment, they opened the Bible together and prayed for an answer. Despite the news, they stood on the foundation of their faith and believed the scripture that says, "nothing is impossible with God." They stood on this promise and believed the bad report was not the end of the matter, but rather the beginning of a miraculous story.

One week after receiving that diagnosis, they were driving to Austin when Caroline felt God tell her to start writing a blog about her journey. She recalls laughing out loud. Since her youth, Caroline had always struggled with writing and reading comprehension. So much so that her parents sent her to a learning center. Caroline also completed all her college English courses at a summer community school, which was much easier than it would have been at Baylor University, where she attended college.

As crazy as writing a blog sounded, she was obedient and followed through. Then things began to shift. What began as a journal of their story slowly turned into a platform where Caroline encouraged other women who were going through infertility, trials, and times of waiting on God. As she became vulnerable and embraced other women's stories, the blog expanded to reach women all over the world! The blog was impactful, so Caroline felt led to start hosting a support group in her living room in June 2013. She started by spreading the word through her church and a few acquaintances. Before she knew it, women who were similarly struggling through infertility began to show up. Many experienced a breakthrough in their lives. Women were able to overcome the shame and stigma of being barren. They could even pray out loud about it for the first time. They received hope, hearts were healed, and women were getting pregnant! They continued to meet, and soon many new women became exposed to Caroline's amazing group, Moms in the Making. In 2015, growth continued. Moms in the Making launched into new territory and reached a new online audience.

Caroline's ministry and vision continued to expand, and in 2016 she wrote her first book, *In Due Time*. That's right, the girl who struggled writing and reading became a published author! *In Due Time* is a sixty-day devotional written to encourage anyone who needs hope and encouragement while they wait on a circumstance to change or to see a dream fulfilled. Caroline's blog and Moms in the Making both had grown so much, she suddenly felt God was leading her into giving up her eleven-year career as a financial analyst. She left the comfort and stability that came with her job and resigned to become a full-time minister to women!

Colby and Caroline had still not had a child of their own, yet their labor of love in caring for other families was growing their spiritual family in ways they could never have imagined. Caroline hosted her first Moms in the Making Conference, which was attended by 160 women from three different countries and thirty-two different states! She also started groups in other cities, and in just a few short years Moms in the Making had grown from eight groups (in 2018) to seventy groups currently across the country. Moms in the Making also has two new Spanish-speaking virtual groups and launched two Dutch-speaking groups in 2021. While tirelessly and passionately pursuing all that God has for her, Caroline launched a podcast in 2019 called A Cup Full of Hope—another platform to bring hope and encouragement to the world!

Here's a recent update from Caroline for 2022: *Colby and I are still trusting the Lord for babies. Through a cancer diagnosis Colby received, the sudden loss of his dad, and our two-year-old nephew losing a battle with brain cancer, we still cling to God's Word and the hope that is available through Jesus! We are expecting to be expecting, and while awaiting our turn we have celebrated over 500 miracle babies that were born from once-barren wombs! Even more so, we have celebrated hearts healed and marriages restored. Women who were once bitter, jealous, fearful, and depressed are now walking in peace and joy. We have hundreds of testimonies documented of the miracles God has provided through the ministry. It's been amazing to be a part of lives being changed! I think about how the trajectory of our life is COMPLETELY different because we didn't have kids "when we* *wanted them." While we desire deeply to be parents, we are so thankful for what God has done these past 10 years!*

Colby and Caroline have truly given their pain a purpose. Now, their vision continues to grow. Colby recently felt God was prompting him to give up his long-term law enforcement career as a special agent to help Caroline form a support system for men going through the infertility journey. Once again, they are stepping out in faith, taking a risk, and leaving comfort behind. Colby and Caroline are a shining example of living their lives **Big, Bold, and Brave**! It is my honor to share their story. You can connect with Caroline by visiting in-due-time.com/connect or by emailing her at trustinginduetime@gmail.com.

The next story I will share is about my friend Robert Kasozi. Very few people reading this will be able to fathom the horror he faced. It's an honor to share a snapshot of his life.

Robert Kasozi

Towering papyrus reeds cracked and split as I crawled through the dense swamp. Feeling crazed and too afraid to stop, I pushed on, fleeing for my life. Gunfire popped sporadically in the distance as I fled towards the hiding places of a desperate group of villagers, who like me, were using the papyrus swamp as a refuge. In my panic, I barely noticed my torn and bare knees, hands, and feet. My thoughts were not on the disease-ridden mosquitoes and tsetse flies, poisonous snakes, or the other dangers the swamp held, and I tried to ignore the bloated corpses floating in the murky water I crawled past as I plunged deeper into the swamp. My only hope was that the soldiers who were trying to kill me were too afraid to enter this dense, putrid death trap. Desperate to survive, I waded deeper into the swamp. Before long swamp slime covered most of my body, making me look more like a hideous swamp creature than a 10-year-old

Ugandan boy. In my worst nightmares, I could not have imagined that I would call this treacherous sanctuary home for the next two and a half years.

Excerpt from Chapter One – Kasozi: The Redemptive Journey of a Ugandan Genocide Survivor. Written by Ruth Marie Hamill and Robert Kasozi, 2021.

I met my dear friend Robert in May 2011. I was in Uganda to be a guest speaker at a five-day youth conference hosted at Seguka Worship Center. At the time, Robert was the pastor of Masulita Worship Center.

In meeting Robert for the first time, I was immediately affected by his sweet, gentle spirit and contagious smile. We discussed many subjects as he took me on a tour of Masulita and provided me some historical context about Uganda. His high intelligence, sense of humor, and thoughtfulness were immediately evident. What I was not prepared for was to hear his story of surviving the Ugandan genocide in the mid-eighties. It was impossible to fathom. How could a child who'd suffered so greatly in such horrific conditions be the same kind, loving man I found myself riding along with? I consider him one of the most amazing humans I've ever met. I cherish the opportunities I have had to see him on rare occasions and Zoom calls. His accomplishments are nothing short of astounding.

Robert has been the pastor of Kawempe Worship Center—a large church with a massive impact in the lives of the community—since 2011. In 2016, Robert took on another role. Following a tragic car accident that took the life of his dear friends and pastors Ed Pohlreich, Scott Volz, and the chairman of UCOM (Uganda Christian Ministry Outreach), Steven Kaweesa, Robert was asked to succeed Kaweesa as the chairman of UCOM. He had been serving as the vice chairman under Pastor Steven. This critical position came with tremendous responsibility, including the unenviable task of succeeding his dear friend, mentor, and revered leader. Robert has been up to the task. He is the perfect leader for the evolving future of UCOM.

Over the years (and through a special partnership), UCOM and WOMF (World Outreach Ministry Foundation) have planted over 350 churches, 270 in Uganda alone. They currently have church plants in Kenya, Tanzania, Rwanda, Burundi, Congo, South Sudan, and Ghana. These churches not only share the Gospel, but they also bring life, medicine, friendship, and hope to the villages they impact. Additionally, they have established twenty-four Yesu Akwagala primary schools, one high school, two Bible colleges, and a prison ministry reaching sixty-two prisons. The UCOM organization in Uganda has grown to employ 205 full-time workers. They continue to expand and provide opportunities to countless individuals.

Since the unimaginable atrocities of the regimes led by Edi Amin and Milton Obote, Uganda has undergone healing as a nation. Tribes that were once bitter, ruthless enemies have set in motion a life-changing time of healing and reconciliation that is still affecting Uganda today. Robert suffered the most under the regime of Obote. Understandably, when Robert was young, he had a hatred of Obote and his participation in the genocide that plagued Uganda. Robert had suffered unthinkable trauma. In 2005, Obote died in exile at the age of eighty-five. It would have been natural for Robert to feel relief in hearing the news of his death, if not even a semblance of celebration and justice. But that is not Kasozi. Robert has experienced incredible healing with the help of God, many mentors, and the powerful act of forgiving others. Here was his reaction to Obote's death in his own words:

> *When I learned Obote had passed, I felt sorrow. I was truly glad to learn his children and their children are good people and doing well. The only way for Uganda to move forward and thrive is to put the past behind it and to forgive and live without offense. Forgiveness is not easy, especially when the offense was so severe and the price so high, but the cost of unforgiveness is much higher. I knew that hatred and unforgiveness would destroy not only me, but my family and ultimately, my country. I chose to forgive.*

Excerpt from Chapter Sixteen – Kasozi: The Redemptive Journey of a Ugandan Genocide Survivor. *Written by Ruth Marie Hamill and Robert Kasozi, 2021*

Robert Kasozi has lived a life far beyond our family mantra of being **Big, Bold, and Brave**. His courage to traverse through his own pain into a place of healing and love for humanity is incredible. I implore you to order his book and read the full story. It will inspire and challenge you in ways you never imagined. You will learn that the human spirit, through a relationship with our Creator, can truly overcome unfathomable fear and pain—and turn it into a catalyst to change the world.

Trials are opportunities to make courageous decisions and release hope to empower others.

Chapter 10 Reflection

I want to help kickstart some ideas for giving *your* pain a purpose. Here are some for you to consider. My list assumes the premise that these ideas focus on breathing *life* into yourself and others.

Loss of a loved one:

- Donate monthly or annually to a cause your loved one was passionate about.

- Start a foundation to raise awareness or prevent someone else from suffering a similar loss. An example is M.A.D.D, or an organization for a specific disease that needs funding and research.

- Join or start a support group or organization that helps people work through their loss.

- Write a book or start a blog to help others!

- Start a podcast to help others.

- Start a YouTube channel and create videos focused on mental health, hope, and embracing the future.

Personal tragedy or disappointment:

- Serve organizations to help others who have suffered in a way you have experienced, such as:

    - Losing their home/possessions in a natural disaster (fire, flood, hurricane, tornado, etc.).

    - Anti-bullying.

- Serving and supporting veterans suffering from PTSD and who have had a hard time acclimating back into civilian life. OR support the family left behind if they died in service.

- Start or join a support group or organization that helps the family of a first responder who lost their life.

- Start a foundation that helps fund/support small business owners who need a fresh start after losing their business because of the pandemic or a natural cause.

- Help those who've lost their careers to start new ones.

- Start or join an organization that supports people suffering from the fall out of divorce, abortion, foster care, or abuse (physical, emotional, sexual).

- Adopt a child.

Chapter 11
What Do You Really Want?

Experiencing a significant loss can cause you to analyze every aspect of your life. It was true for us. Examining our priorities came first. Don't get me wrong, we had *stated* our priorities, but this new season would force us to look at whether we were really *living* according to those priorities! It's easy to say things like, "Family comes first, I am going to build a new business, and we are going to take a two-week family vacation every year!" We don't always execute those plans for the simple reason that our plans are too vague. We have goals without a system or process to achieve them. We waste time doing things that don't take us where we want to go, and which often steal our physical, emotional, and spiritual energy.

There are a lot of great books on how to change habits and create new behaviors. *Atomic Habits* (by James Clear) and *The Power of Habit* (by Charles Duhigg) are two of my current favorites for helping with the "how to" of change. In this chapter, I am going to focus on what changed for us, aided us in the healing process, and what allowed us to experience a more fulfilling life even during our grieving process. I will do so by presenting you with a life *philosophy*.

> *Living a Big, Bold, and Brave life requires the willingness and vulnerability to admit there are areas in our lives that we are not satisfied with and that it is our fault they're that way.*

You may have great success in an area of your life right now. Maybe you're very successful in business and have achieved great financial wealth, but your marriage and family are broken, your friendships suck, and you don't take care of your body or emotional health. Or maybe you have great relationships but struggle financially. There are a million combinations for having a deficit in your life satisfaction. The reason is likely quite simple: you have done nothing intentional to change it! That was us. Losing our oldest son became the spark that caused us to reevaluate … *everything*!

Our starting point was to prioritize things that brought us energy and joy. That required some honest and sometimes emotional conversations between Amárillys and me. This may sound like an obvious and easy step. However, it's actually one of the hardest, most foundational steps.

Why? Let me explain.

I have been coaching individuals and couples for almost twenty years. And I've been thrust into situations where the person or couple is in crisis mode. The world is falling apart all around them. Sometimes there are core emotional issues and trauma that require the attention of a professional therapist. But the most common threat I have seen that causes destruction in relationships and building the life we desire is this: unmet or unspoken expectations.

For various reasons, this discussion can be especially difficult in a marriage or relationship. It can lead to one side blaming the other for why expectations haven't been met. Tones are often accusatory in this case, and an accusation can hit like a sledgehammer—particularly if it involves something you've never discussed. The accused feels blindsided. A responding argument often ensues about not having the ability to read people's thoughts. "How could you not know?" the accuser demands. Sound familiar, anyone? Emotions tend to flare from a flicker to a scorching flame when unspoken expectations arise.

And even if an unmet expectation is communicated in a loving, kind way, one side frequently gets defensive and tries to deflect from why they are not responsible for the outcome. They run through a laundry list of all the expectations they feel confident they *have* met. They may respond, "Give me a break! What about ____ and ____? It seems what I do around here is never enough!" I've been tried and found guilty of such a defense. Typically, it's because I was aware of the unmet expectation, at least on some level, but didn't act on the change necessary to meet it. What's worse, I may have sensed it without needing a cue, but chose not to bring the potential unmet expectation to the surface in conversation. I did this either because I didn't want to look bad or to avoid conflict and find a way to sneak in meeting the expectation *later*. But *later* rarely comes if things are not openly discussed. The results are the same in both scenarios.

During the nearly two decades we've been together, Amárillys and I have experienced challenges discussing expectations. We've generally navigated them in healthy ways. With Gabriel's death, we sensed there was an urgency to put everything on the table. We were determined to work through our pain and start a new journey. So, we began picking apart our values, priorities, unmet and unspoken expectations, dreams, goals, and frustrations. As she likes to say, we examined "all the things."

Unmet expectations can take many forms. Here's a sample list:

Job/Career:

My boss or co-workers don't show me appreciation.

I am not valued for the work I do and what I bring to the table.

I am not growing or engaging my true talents or what I am passionate about.

I hate my work schedule. I work too many hours, or my schedule prevents me from doing the things I consider a higher priority.

My employer doesn't pay me enough.

Marriage:

We are so focused on prioritizing our kids, there is little room for each other.

Our romantic flame has dwindled; we are more like roommates/friends than a married couple.

We don't make enough household income.

My spouse battles long-term health issues.

My spouse has put on excessive weight.

My spouse is not romantic.

My wife never wears sexy clothing, only yoga pants and oversized pajama bottoms! My husband has poor hygiene and wears t-shirts he wore back in college!

Our sex life is not satisfying. It lacks quality and quantity. Either it was never great, or we have stopped pursuing it.

We appear to have two separate visions for our marriage. How can we continue to walk together?

We can't have truthful conversations without them ending in a fight. Instead of coming to an understanding, we both feel the other is not listening and that they are *wrong*.

One or both partners have allowed their dreams and desires to go dormant.

Relationships:

I have no intimate friendships.

I am so busy with my job, there is no time to meet new people and make friends.

I am so busy with my job, there is no time to find someone to share my life with.

I always lose myself and end up doing what other people want me to do.

I always get burned by people.

I am not appreciated and/or valued by my family or friends.

Personal Growth:

I have been through terrible things in my past that haunt my future.

I never had a chance to pursue my education or what I really wanted to do in life.

I had such a wonderful past, but my present and future are bleak in comparison. My best days are behind me.

I typically see hurdles and challenges, not solutions or opportunities.

I have goals, but I feel they are more like pipedreams.

I can't help the way I am because _____.

Physical Health and Body:

I was dealt bad genes. My condition is out of my control.

I am too tall, short, skinny, fat, or ugly.

I can't afford to eat healthy food; it's too expensive.

I have tried to get healthy before and I failed.

You might add some things to this list. The point is, when unmet expectations continue long enough, they can eventually turn into *unspoken* expectations. And at that point, they get truly dangerous. You position yourself for potential lifelong disappointment and internal struggle because you'll refuse to even talk about and address how you can make a change.

For some, it only takes one major hit in life—perhaps a single statement made by a parent, relative, teacher, or close friend that provokes us into burying what we really want out of life. You may learn to pretend you don't have unmet expectations while below the surface they are mingling with the root of bitterness. Bitter people lead miserable lives.

In other cases, an accumulation of unmet expectations stacks up like a pile of bricks. But they all have one massive thing in common: THEY DON'T HAVE TO STAY UNMET! In many cases, lies have blinded you from seeing the truth: You've had the ability to meet your unfulfilled expectations all along.

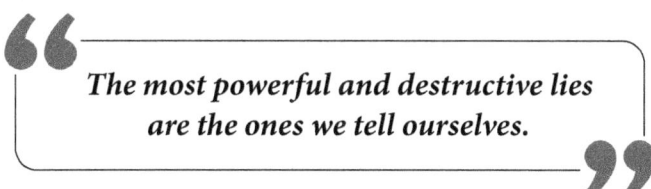

The most powerful and destructive lies are the ones we tell ourselves.

In my case, I had some unmet expectations. For many years I wanted to start a business, create new streams of income, coach people outside of my church position, travel more, and have more fun with my family. I had allowed other people's opinions of my abilities and potential to stop me from doing what I *REALLY wanted* to do. Sure, I tried to be faithful in my roles, and I had some great times. Yet there was always a burning ember to do more. It was very close to being extinguished at times. But it remained in there, smoldering.

That ember is in you too. What unmet expectations do you keep? Make a list right now while the iron is hot. Write whatever comes to mind in the next five minutes. Set a timer. I'll wait!

Whether you followed my instruction or not, I asked you to confront your unmet expectations for one reason. There is hope. You don't have to remain stuck in a tar pit of disappointment or loss! Change does require something of you, though. There's an adage we are probably all familiar with: *The definition of insanity is doing the same thing and expecting different results.* First, you must bring to the surface and identify the things you want to change. What do you *WANT* out of life? Once that's settled, act on it!! This rule applied to me. It applied to Amárillys. We made changes. It applies to you too.

One thing Amárillys and I both wanted was to be in better physical shape. We had been working out consistently for about a year prior to Gabriel's crash. The trauma and heavy grief in the initial days after his death made working out impossible, so we took a break. After a month or so, we recognized that we would be in intense grief for an undetermined amount of time. We knew that if we allowed our bodies to become weak, it would exacerbate the struggle in our mind and soul. Then, a few short months after Gabriel's death, COVID arrived. With it dominating the world, we knew getting as healthy as possible was more important than ever.

We upped our commitment to a healthy and fit lifestyle. If we were going to change our lives, we had to start paying more attention to our overall spiritual, mental, emotional, *and* physical condition. There are countless studies pointing to the importance of exercise and being as lean as your natural body type will allow. And no, I'm not talking about becoming an elite bodybuilder or athlete. They *train*. If you're one of those, wonderful. I'm simply referring to valuing your health and moving your body!

What's more, exercising a minimum of three days a week for at least thirty minutes with an increased heart rate has tremendous health benefits. Exercising, when combined with maintaining a healthy diet, is critical in building a healthy immune system, strong muscles, bones, and improving your general well-being. Also, studies from neuroscientists illustrate the benefits of exercise for your *brain*. Working out your body vastly improves your brain, memory, and creative function. We work out together six days a week, with one rest day. Not because that's better or necessary—but because we *really want* to.

One thing that topped Amárillys' list of unmet expectations was having more fun in our marriage and as a family. It was on my list too! I was also the biggest barrier for that one coming to fruition.

I loved having fun. Heck, when I was in my teens and twenties, I was often considered the life of the party. I'm sure we have some current friends and acquaintances who might be surprised by this because they have rarely seen flashes of me being the fun instigator. What happened to *that* guy? Why had planning for and having fun become so difficult for me? It was a valid unmet expectation for Amárillys and only a *stated* expectation for me. It had to change, and it was up to me to act.

I dug deep to unearth what had started me down the path of being the "unfun" guy in the household. I believe I discovered the answer. I became a Christian in 1997. Fun guy began to die. Let me explain. I wasn't just the fun guy prior to having a relationship with God. I was also often irresponsible. Sure, I always had a job and paid my bills. But I was never serious about my future.

When I became a Christian, I decided that would have to change. I became *serious*—dead serious. I wore my new cloak of responsibility like a badge of honor. I didn't notice that my ability to have fun and enjoy the moment was decaying. But it did. I became overwhelmed with a sense of responsibility, and even though I could still have bursts of fun and laughter, they became more infrequent. If asked to describe me today in one word, most people—and certainly my bride—would say *intense*. A kind way of saying I am not always a fun guy.

In looking back at how I approached life (specifically how I embraced my role as a pastor in the organizations I was part of) I strove to be the most responsible guy in the building. I am a hard worker and have always taken pride in doing a good job, going back to my very first job at sixteen years old. Working hard and taking on more responsibility than you should is one thing—abdicating your dreams and desires is another.

A few years ago, I held a staff position that was killing me from the inside out. I had allowed myself to carry responsibilities that were not mine. I said yes to way too many things. I didn't want to be doing what I was doing. Worse, I didn't see anywhere in the organization I *wanted* to grow into. I found myself going through the motions, feeling like I was trapped. The parade of meetings, events, programs, and the uncertainty of how I fit into the organization's future had become a concrete weight around my neck. I was very unhappy with our rhythm of life.

Maybe you relate? Here's the rub (it may feel like sandpaper), which you may not agree with or like. My dissatisfaction with life wasn't the organization's fault. Or the people in it. Yes, if I had more authority, I would have changed a few things that frustrated me, but it wouldn't have been enough. The truth was, I wanted to try something new. I *always* had a *choice*! No one put a gun to my head. No one put limits on me I couldn't shake free of. I put them on myself and allowed what I really wanted to be overshadowed by feeling responsible to help other people pursue what they wanted at my expense. I made a radical decision. I walked away from a well-paying position and our comfort in search of something different. Amárillys and I were in complete agreement, and we felt like God was too.

Once we stepped into our new adventure, I was determined to be less intense and have more fun. I would be more spontaneous. I took baby steps. As I mentioned before, this slippery slope started when I became a Christian. But I'd like to mention that my decision to form a relationship with Jesus is the single greatest I have ever made, and it has been the source of great joy and peace in my life for the last twenty-five years. He is not the reason I became too serious or didn't chase my dreams. The inability to allow "fun guy" to coexist with being a mature, responsible adult lied solely with me.

I was deceived into thinking that being serious—okay, *intense*—was somehow a sign of Godliness. Creating a new rhythm in our lives helped me start to break that pattern. It's still a challenge to be more relaxed and have more fun. No one is ready to declare me Mr. Spontaneity just yet. But I have made strides. I take myself far less seriously these days, and I'm far more aware of when I needlessly slip into Mr. Intensity.

Several months into our new adventure, I had not taken many steps towards doing what I outlined earlier. I had yet to start a coaching business, develop new streams of income, or travel more. The rhythm of life had changed, but I was still averse to taking the risks necessary to pursue what I said I really wanted. My mindset was slowly changing. The smoldering ember had become a small flame. Then Gabriel died. After the first year of wading through the grieving process while also dealing with a world turned upside down by a virus, a "suddenly" occurred. Even though our exact future appeared foggy, I could see clearly at the same time. Reflecting on how Gabriel lived brought about a realization.

> *It took losing my teenage son to shake me out of the coma of mediocrity I was in. It was time to stop being a coward!*

It was time to fully live out the phrase that Gabriel inspired. I had to live **Big, Bold, and Brave** and start doing, not just saying.

Amárillys and I had long, open discussions regarding what filled our calendar and what didn't. Specifically, we discussed what activities brought us joy and what we wished we did more often. Then we identified some things we wished to do less or eliminate entirely. Once we had narrowed those things, we began to strategize how we could do more of what we wanted and less of the mundane.

This is not as easy as it sounds. It involves how we prioritize our interactions with other people. But it's necessary. We have choices, and the choice is ours alone to make. As I said, traveling was one thing on top of our "do more" list.

The last two years have not been the easiest for world travel. Fear and various restrictions in certain cities and states here in the U.S., and in countries around the globe, have limited the options. Then there were mask mandates on planes, tension between passengers and crew, and friction between passengers. It doesn't dissuade us. None of those things will stop us.

I turned fifty-five in December 2020. So, Amárillys challenged me to partake in fifty-five adventures during the year. She was doing her part to try and kill "unfun" guy. Since my birthday is in mid-December, starting 2021 off with a bang was a must! We began with a trip to stay with Amárillys' dad and mom-in-love in Orlando for New Year's.

I haven't mentioned this yet—Amárillys is a full-blooded Puerto Rican. She doesn't have a flag hanging from her rearview mirror or a bumper sticker, but make no mistake, she is an island girl!

If you have never been to a party hosted by Puerto Ricans, you need to find some Boricua friends right now. Seriously, they know how to throw parties. We were there for the entire New Year's week, provided with a few days of music, dancing, karaoke, roasted pig (lechón asado), the works! For the record, I don't eat much pork aside from bacon. But if you have never had a full-sized pig Puerto-Rican-style (meaning lathered and massaged in garlic, oil, and other heavenly spices, then cooked *very* slowly in the backyard inside a Chinese Oven, which is a version of a homemade fire pit that comes in a box), you have no idea what you're missing. It's amazing! The meat falls off the bone and melts in your mouth! Each party we attended (there were several hosted by various Puerto Rican friends) had its own unique flare. We had a blast!

It was the perfect start to a year of fifty-five adventures. And not all adventures had to be epic. My adventures included going places with my father-in-law, Santos. These were not qualified adventures because of the destination or what we would do when we arrived, but because *he was driving*. Santos loves nice sports cars. He also thinks of speed limits and lanes as mere suggestions. If you have ever driven on the roads in Puerto Rico, you know. I knocked out several of the 55 adventures just running errands with him! In years past, there were many reasons why we would not have taken the time and expense to make this trip. We were finally doing what we *really wanted* to do!

Our adventures continued throughout 2021. Amárillys and I went on some one-night and weekend trips close by for short, personal marriage retreats. One of those crazy adventures was during the now infamous *Snowmageddon* in the Dallas area. We attended a Valentine's event that was supposed to be a weekend of dining and dancing, when suddenly the hotel lost its ability to supply heat. The hotel soon became an ice box, and many of the activities were shut down.

There was no food that Saturday for the attendees, so we volunteered to go pick some up. We were already familiar with the area, and I was confident I could drive safely in the snow. We went all over town in subfreezing weather trying to gather enough supplies to bring back. It sounds miserable, but we had so much fun and laughed along the way! After all, we were out doing what we *really wanted* to do!

The Snowmageddon adventure continued when we returned home with the boys and found a house without power. Yes, we had another choice to make—be angry and frustrated, or turn the misfortune into an adventure. Adventures are more fun. We kept warm by bundling up in the living room by our gas fireplace. We played games, cooked on our gas stove, and lit the house with several new flashlights I'd picked up at Costco. We played in the snow. The situation wasn't what we would have drawn up, but in it we found ways to do what *we wanted* to do.

Noticing a theme? For our anniversary we traveled to Mexico despite the threat of being quarantined if we tested positive before our return flight. Big deal! It was totally worth the risk. We had a great time. We were doing what *we wanted* to do. Fear and inconveniences were not going to stop us.

That summer, we organized a family trip to a beautiful cabin in Broken Bow, Oklahoma. We spent time hiking, boating, and eating with some dear friends who had rented another cabin.

Later that year, we spent a few days before Christmas with the boys at a condo on a lake enjoying a massive hot tub, playing corn hole, drowning worms (I would say fishing, but we didn't catch a thing!), watching movies, and eating snacks. It was exactly what *we wanted* to do.

Now, vacations and getaways are not the only valid expression of doing what you really want to do. There are probably other things more significant and potentially life changing. For you this might mean shifting your career, going after the promotion you think you are not qualified for, starting that business you dreamed of, getting out of toxic relationships, and more.

Let me ask you a question. Have you felt stuck in a rut or paralyzed by the state of our world? We did too. And you know how we changed that? We did something about it! Since the last quarter of 2021, Amárillys and I have traded in our excuses and faulty mindsets for actions and healthy mindsets. We have taken our future by the horns. Yes, we have had to fight through the gauntlet of fears, doubts, and behavioral patterns of the past like everyone else. Every day is not easy, and we still have to do some things we don't really want to. We are just experiencing those much less now, doing more of what we want instead.

I launched my coaching company and brand, **BigBoldBrave**. I wrote this book. I intend to start a podcast, **Stories of Big Bold Brave Humans**. These new ventures are risky, but exciting! I am doing what *I want* to do. I heard someone the other day talking about studies that reveal the following truth: most people regret decisions they *didn't act on* more than things they regret *doing*. Will that be you?

Both of my parents passed away about seven years ago. I learned the value of being an honest person and working hard from them. I honor them for that. However, I will never forget a regret they mentioned a few times over the course of my adult years. When they were a young married couple in the early '60s and '70s, they had opportunities to invest in some Southern California real estate. They were afraid of the possible risk, so they chose not to. Others they knew bet on themselves and are now quite wealthy. Our family's financial trajectory could have been far different. Playing it safe can keep you from realizing your dreams and desires for your family. I am done with playing it safe. What about you?

Amárillys is done too. She started painting a few years ago. She is an amazing talent, and she had no idea until she started sharing her work on Instagram (you can follow her there at art.by.amarillys). People love her artwork. Her paintings and commissioned pieces are selling quickly and have been a major inspiration to her clients, often affecting them in deep, personal ways. She recently launched a website, **ArtbyAmarillys.com**. Being vulnerable and courageous enough to put herself out there and charge money for her work is no small feat. It was scary, but it's been worth the risk. She was recently accepted to be a featured artist at The Other Art Fair in Dallas, TX. This show is presented by SAATCHI ART, the world's leading online gallery for art in partnership with Bombay Sapphire. Three short years ago that was a pipedream!

She also birthed a brainchild she has been sitting on for a few years called **Renaissance Creatives**. It is an event where women gather to allow for unencumbered creative expression. Their creative expression can take many forms, including—but not limited to—the arts. The first event included music and songwriting, painting (of course!), dance, creative writing, poetry, spoken word, cooking and party hosting, and photography. The mission of this event is to explore the creative expression that flows through each woman as she activates the freedom to be authentically who God made her to be. To create *with* God. A creative expression that is uniquely theirs and brings to Earth something that has never been before. The experience is beautiful and powerful.

Renaissance Creatives began to unfold when Amárillys' longtime friend, LeTesha, challenged her to quit thinking about it and act by putting a physical date on the calendar, and then publicize it! Since making that one courageous decision, the vision, plan, team, and resources needed all fell into place. It's amazing what can happen when you start doing what you *want* to do! I believe God begins to breathe life into it. There is a creative nature in all of us that can change the world around us. Whether you are a musician, accountant, artist, psychiatrist, CEO, kindergarten teacher, or anything else, you have a creative nature and ability that is uniquely yours. It takes courage and risk to see it mature into a powerful force.

Life is exciting again. We see opportunities where we once saw routine or closed doors. I hope you're getting the point of why I am sharing what ***we*** *really want* to do. I am hopeful that the lessons from our journey will shake you free from the shackles of fear, worry, and doubt. You have ONE life, and no one gets out of it alive.

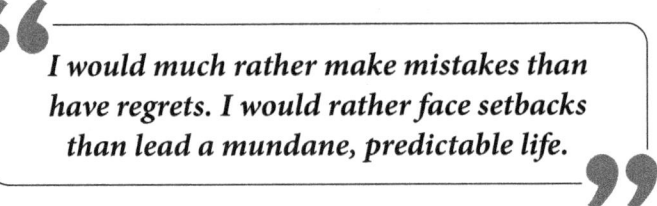

I would much rather make mistakes than have regrets. I would rather face setbacks than lead a mundane, predictable life.

And if you already attack life this way, keep at it and inspire others!

We have not made these changes in a vacuum. We have collaborated with people who bring us joy, energy, and who challenge us with new ideas and ways of thinking. Sometimes they call us to the mat and push us out of our comfort zones. We invite it!

Don't fear taking risks and trying new things. Be afraid of staying the same. Start doing what you want to do and stop blaming others for why you haven't!

There are many things that can steal the joy and energy that make life more fulfilling. Nothing is more influential than the people in your inner circle. They can propel you to greatness or paralyze you into a life of mediocrity. To live **Big, Bold, and Brave**, you will need to examine who you surround yourself with. In *Proverbs*, referred to as the *Book of Wisdom*, Solomon, the wise guy, wrote: "He that walketh with wise men shall be wise: but a companion of fools shall be destroyed." There is a modern-day quote reflecting his thoughts: "Show me your friends and I will show you your future."

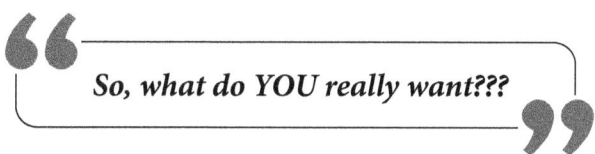

So, what do YOU really want???

The next chapter is short. But for some, it may serve as the most critical takeaway in the book.

Chapter 11 Reflection

List some things you have wanted to do for a long time:

Now, list the obstacles you believe are keeping you from realizing them.

Dig deeper—what lies have you allowed yourself that are now preventing you from overcoming the obstacles and doing what you *really* want to do?

Do you know others who have overcome great odds? You should! Some are in this book! You can overcome the odds you face, too!

What steps or courageous decisions will launch you on a new track towards fulfilling these desires?

Chapter 12
Parasites and Boundaries

> *Eliminate or minimize the relationships that suck the life out of you.*

We all likely have at least one person in our life who has or will become a parasite. We might be that person to someone else. I know that sounds harsh. By Webster's definition, a parasite is *an organism that lives on or in a host organism and gets its food from or at the expense of its host.* I challenge you to ask yourself: Is a friend who insists you be on-demand to ride the emotional rollercoaster of *their* life, tries to manipulate your emotions, has no value for your time, family, or financial resources, and sucks the energy out of you a true *friend*?

We've all encountered toxic humans. It can be very difficult to end a toxic relationship, especially if the toxicity has continued unopposed. I've mentioned that living a life with radical impact requires courageous decisions. Courage is not required to allow a toxic relationship to remain in your life. In fact, doing so requires the opposite: cowardice. I don't like being called a coward, and I'm betting you don't either. It is a word that offends our very being. But it's the correct word to use here. Webster's defines cowardice as: *lack of courage or firmness of purpose*. Ouch.

The degree in which you allow toxic relationships access to your life is the degree you will fall short of living your best life. It's impossible to befriend toxicity without it creating drag.

I was watching the Winter Olympics a couple of weeks ago. One of my favorite events is the Super-G downhill race. Skiers typically reach speeds of 80 mph, and in some cases even faster for short bursts. The broadcast did a feature on the special suits Team USA was wearing at these Olympics. They cost $1,000 *each*! What's crazier is that they are only worn *once*! Their purpose, and the justifiable reason for the budget expense, is speed! They make the skiers more aerodynamic. We need to manage our relationships like we are wearing one of those suits.

Some toxic relationships are easy to spot. Others are stealth. It's important to occasionally evaluate the quality of the people we grant access to our inner circle. Sometimes we get stuck in relationships we feel we must stay in. Guess what? You don't have to stay. "But you don't understand my situation," you say. I don't have to. If you are allowing people to control your life and sacrifice yours for theirs, that's on *you*.

In the wake of Gabriel's death, we had a very limited capacity to be around people. And by people, I mean *anyone*. The pandemic amplified this. At the same time, we realized it wouldn't be healthy to isolate ourselves. For our mental and emotional health, we began to analyze who we spent our time with and how often we spent time with them. A quick litmus test is to examine how often you feel encouraged, supported, or energized by being around the people in your life. Here's the criteria Amárillys and I use for evaluating relationships:

Does the relationship energize us? If so, you won't struggle at the thought of spending time with them.

Do we have fun together? Do they make us laugh or bring us joy? If not, why are we hanging out?

Are they helping *us* grow, personally or as a couple?

Have we developed enough trust to give them permission to challenge us when we exhibit behavior that does not fit the character we desire to personify?

Do they inspire us to think outside the box and ponder new ideas?

Are we mutually fascinated with each other? In other words, are we excited to share what's going on with our lives, encourage each other, and ask questions? Are conversations two-way and not one-sided?

Do we respect one another and value each other's time and commitments?

Here's a big one. When the chips are down, are they one of the first calls we would make?

Do we share a common cause or vision in some capacity?

You can think of others.

Mentoring relationships are an entirely different category. Amárillys and I have coached and mentored many people over the years. In those relationships, we learned some important questions to ask ourselves. Did *the person* want to grow more than *we* wanted them to grow? Were we more committed to their success than they were? If we discovered certain actions could improve someone's life or situation, did they execute them, or did they make excuses for why they didn't act on them?

People will prove if they really want mentorship by the actions and behavioral changes they make, not by constantly pointing the finger at others and complaining about their life. This type of person has a victim mentality. They blame everyone and everything for their issues and circumstances. They refuse to take personal responsibility for the life they have created. You can't help them until they are ready for change.

We don't have much room for a victim mentality in our personal life. Again, please don't misunderstand me here. We still meet with people who are in crisis or are struggling if we feel they are someone we should try to help. But we don't feel responsible to help everyone that asks, and we never feel responsible *for* them. It's not our role to save the world, and it's not yours either. Our personal life is a different story. It is sacred. We choose our intimate friendships wisely. You should too. Even with family.

I understand we can't always eliminate toxic family members. Doing so might require murder, which is generally frowned upon. However, that does not mean a toxic family member should be afforded free 24/7 access into our life. It doesn't mean we need to be subject to their every whim, do things their way, or answer every 2 a.m. phone call. There is one truth we must understand about toxic people with no boundaries: They will never be the one to initiate building healthy boundaries!

> *Make a courageous decision. Detoxify the relationships you can't eliminate by setting boundaries and minimizing their ability to pollute your life.*

By Webster's definition, a boundary *is something that marks a limit or extent.* In relation to boundaries for a relationship, it's where you end and someone else begins. There should be a clear distinction on both sides. Let's say you're a rancher and you keep livestock. Imagine a physical border (like a fence) that you build around your property. The fence has a dual purpose. One is to keep the livestock *inside* and safe. The other is to keep harmful intruders *out*.

Now imagine you're a breeder of purebred Tibetan Mastiffs, the world's most expensive breed at an average price of $2,000 per dog. One eleven-month-old sold for a whopping $1.6 million in recent years. You would make darn sure you have a very secure fence to keep your prized females inside. You would install every measure possible to keep a stray male from gaining access, impregnating one of your dogs, and creating a crossbreed. A strange analogy? No. It's very accurate.

Without boundaries, we begin to crossbreed with other humans. Before we know it, we can begin to adopt others' toxic mindsets, degraded value systems, burdens, anxieties, fears, and more.

We can even confuse our true passions and chase the wrong dreams.

I'll never forget a story I heard at a leadership seminar I attended back in 1998 when I was an Independent Distributor for Symmetry International, a health and wellness products company. One of the executive vice presidents shared a story from his longtime friendship with another executive in the company (we'll call them Bill and Fred). The fellow colleague, Fred, was a licensed pilot. One day they went for a ride in Fred's plane. Fred was very passionate about flying. He raved about the benefits of having your own plane, the freedoms it allowed, avoiding the hassle and extra hours of flying commercial, flying to a destination just to have lunch, and so on. His exuberance was contagious. So contagious, in fact, that Bill began to pursue earning his pilot's license! He spent thousands of dollars and hours investing in this new venture. That is, until he had a sober moment while on a training flight. Suddenly, Bill thought, "What am I doing?"

He reasoned with himself that he did **not** want to become a pilot, nor did he like flying his own plane! He consciously began to refute all the benefits his passionate friend had convinced him of about being a private pilot. He concluded, "There are planes that go all over the world, and I can afford first class tickets." His final thought was, "Why am I going to all this work and expense when I don't even like it!" Bill quit pursuing his Pilot's License that day!

Sound extreme? Well, if we get pulled in by other people's passions in a healthy friendship, is it not possible and more dangerous to get pulled into another human's dysfunction? Without boundaries in our relationships, chaos ensues. We begin to take on the character and traits of others, often unwittingly. I'll give you another real-life, simple example. We have counseled marriages for many years. The marriages were often in crisis mode or very dysfunctional. Early on in our experience working with couples, we noticed a phenomenon. There were sessions when emotions were intense, and there would be a complete breakdown in communication between the husband and wife. We would help with what we could, then leave. On the ride home (or later that day), we would find ourselves in an argument or unable to communicate effectively. We quickly recognized the pattern. The spirit of the couple's communication and dysfunction would temporarily become ours—that is, until we recognized and dealt with it. We trained many leaders on our marriage ministry teams to look out for this.

The remedy for defending against someone else's dysfunction was and is simple. After a meeting, we would talk about what happened between the distressed couple. We'd identify ways their spirit, emotions, or actions were causing disconnection and/or a breakdown of communication (anger, disrespect, having an affair, selfishness, fear, distrust, an unwillingness to forgive, suspicion, etc.). We would finish by saying a simple prayer and declaring healthy characteristics over our marriage that were counter to what the couple released into the atmosphere. We discovered it worked instantly, every time.

That method has allowed us to help countless couples over the years without us ingesting their poison. I am using a vivid example here to make a point about something I believe you should never allow! If you knew someone was slipping a little strychnine into your bottled water, would you drink it? Don't allow people to slip poison into your mind, spirit, and emotions either! It's okay to walk away from toxic relationships!

That said, I also have a personal ethic: I always keep a lane on the highway of relationships open *back to me*. In other words, if the toxic person starts taking responsibility and shows growth, I am always open to reconciliation in some form (unless the case is extreme).

If you don't build boundaries and learn to identify the parasites in your life, you will never become the most powerful, healthy version of yourself. Intruders will have full access, and you will be a different person as a result. If this resonates with you at all, then you must act, now! Don't wait. If you need help setting boundaries, perhaps you should hire a coach, see a therapist, incorporate the help of a trusted friend, or read one of the many books on the subject. No matter what, PLEASE ESTABLISH HEALTHIER BOUNDARIES!

CHAPTER 12 REFLECTION

Let's finish with a simple yet revealing exercise. It has been well known for decades that the level of success and fulfillment you will reach in life is directly correlated to our top five Inner Circle relationships (meaning those we spend the most time with and who have the most influence in our life). We need to evaluate those relationships and see where adjustments may be needed.

Step One: List your top five relationships (could include couples). Use the questions on page 157 to evaluate the quality of the relationship, give the person +1 point for each question the answer is "yes", and give them -1 point for the questions the answer is "no". Add up the total for each person. Scores will range from anywhere between -9 to a high of +9. A score of 6+ or above is a healthy, quality relationship.

Step Two: Think of five people (could include couples) you wish you could spend more time with. Score them the same way using the evaluating questions.

Step Three: Compare the final scores of each relationship. Do any of your current top five score poorly compared to your second list of five?

Step Four: By this point, you should have a clear picture of:

- Which people are quality relationships and worth the investment in your life.
- Who in your top five you should consider replacing (and perhaps even a relationship that should be discontinued entirely).

People in your *second group of five* that have high scores would be ideal to replace someone in your *first group of five*.

My Why

I WAS GIVEN BEAUTIFUL advice from Howard Behar, who wrote the foreword, before I started writing this book. He said, "Write this book with the goal of helping *one* person." I hope that person is *you*. You may be very successful and influential in your own right, or you may be struggling to get off the ground and take flight. Our world needs an influx of courageous people—those who possess a deep love and value for all humans—to lead the way during uncertain times. These heroes will have at least a few things in common. Each will have a disdain for allowing fear to dictate their lives. They will choose to give their pain a purpose and use it as a catalyst to uplift others. They'll carry hope and see opportunities where others are hopeless and only see closed doors. And they will continue bravely living vulnerable, authentic lives that inspire others to join them in the journey. This world needs YOU!

Amárillys and I don't consider our life experiences to be unique, nor do we see ourselves as unusually heroic. One thing I can say with confidence is that this book is not theoretical. It describes the principles and values we strive to live by every day. We fall short at times. Many humans face greater challenges with truly heroic results. I think there is a hero in everyone waiting to break out, and there are stories to be told that will inspire people to live with nobler motives. If this book resonates with you and you desire to be a part of our community, I am thrilled. The vision for BigBoldBrave is far more ambitious than my personal development coaching brand. My desire is to connect with like-minded people like you, collaborate, and help you share *your* story. Together we can inspire and change the world!

If this book helped you on any level, then it was worth the blood, sweat, and literal tears.

My final admonition should come as no surprise. It is to accept the challenge of creating the biggest, most impactful life possible. Live your life, **Big, Bold, and Brave**!

~ Clint

Last family portrait 2018
Photo Credit: Terra Wagner - Owner/Photographer at Taken By Terra

Clint, Joel, and Liam -
BigBoldBrave Launch 2022

The Hatton family on
Mother's Day 2022

Clint and Amárillys BigBoldBrave Launch 2022

A young Gabriel dreaming of being a pilot

Kevin Lacey instructing Gabriel on one of his first flights

Members of the Tango 31 Clube hanging out with representatives from the National Air Traffic Controllers Association at AirVenture Oshkosh in Oshkosh, Wisconsin July of 2019.

Gabriel performing a tune up to earn "airtime"

*After a successful checkride,
Private Pilot License in hand!
July 2, 2019*

www.ingramcontent.com/pod-product-compliance
Lightning Source LLC
Chambersburg PA
CBHW050905160426
43194CB00011B/2294